User Stories Applied

User Stories Applied

for Agile Software Development

Mike Cohn

♠ Addison-Wesley

Boston • San Francisco • New York • Toronto • Montreal
London • Munich • Paris • Madrid
Capetown • Sydney • Tokyo • Singapore • Mexico City

The publisher offers discounts on this book when ordered in quantity for bulk purchases and special sales. For more information, please contact:

U.S. Corporate and Government Sales
(800) 382-3419
corpsales@pearsontechgroup.com

For sales outside of the U.S., please contact:

International Sales
(317) 581-3793
international@pearsontechgroup.com

Visit Addison-Wesley on the Web: www.awprofessional.com

Library of Congress Cataloging-in-Publication Data

A catalog record for this book can be obtained from the Library of Congress

ISBN 0-321-20568 5
Text printed on recycled paper
First printing, February 2004

To Laura, for reading this one;
To Savannah, for loving to read;
To Delaney, for insisting you already know how to read.
With readers like you, it's easy to write.

Contents

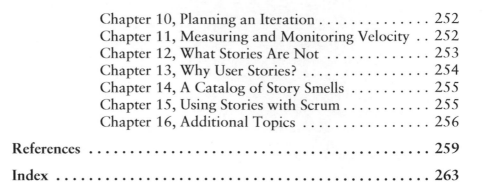

Foreword

How do you decide what a software system is supposed to do? And then, how do you communicate that decision between the various people affected? This book takes on this complicated problem. The problem is difficult because each participant has different needs. Project managers want to track progress. Programmers want to implement the system. Product managers want flexibility. Testers want to measure. Users want a useful system. Creating productive conflict between these perspectives, coming to a single collective decision everyone can support, and maintaining that balance for months or years are all difficult problems.

The solution Mike Cohn explores in this book, *User Stories Applied*, is superficially the same as previous attempts to solve this problem—requirements, use cases, and scenarios. What's so complicated? You write down what you want to do and then you do it. The proliferation of solutions suggests that the problem is not as simple as it appears. The variation comes down to what you write down and when.

User stories start the process by writing down just two pieces of information: each goal to be satisfied by the system and the rough cost of satisfying that goal. This takes just a few sentences and gives you information other approaches don't. Using the principle of the "last responsible moment," the team defers writing down most details of the features until just before implementation.

This simple time shift has two major effects. First, the team can easily begin implementing the "juiciest" features early in the development cycle while the other features are still vague. The automated tests specifying the details of each feature ensure that early features continue to run as specified as you add new features. Second, putting a price on features early encourages prioritizing from the beginning instead of a panicked abortion of scope at the end in order to meet a delivery date.

xvi FOREWORD

Mike's experience with user stories makes this a book full of practical advice for making user stories work for your development team. I wish you clear, confident development.

Kent Beck
Three Rivers Institute

Acknowledgments

This book has benefitted greatly from comments from many reviewers. In particular I thank Marco Abis, Dave Astels, Steve Bannerman, Steve Berczuk, Lyn Bain, Dan Brown, Laura Cohn, Ron Crocker, Ward Cunningham, Rachel Davies, Robert Ellsworth, Doris Ford, John Gilman, Sven Gorts, Deb Hartmann, Chris Leslie, Chin Keong Ling, Phlip, Keith Ray, Michele Sliger, Jeff Tatelman, Anko Tijman, Trond Wingård, Jason Yip, and a handful of anonymous reviewers.

My sincerest thanks to my formal reviewers: Ron Jeffries, Tom Poppendieck, and Bill Wake. Ron kept me honest and agile. Tom opened my eyes to many ideas I hadn't considered before. Bill kept me on track and shared with me his INVEST acronym. This book has been immeasurably improved by suggestions from each of these fine individuals with whom I am proud to have worked.

I also thank Lisa Crispin, author of *Testing Extreme Programming*, who encouraged me to write this book by telling me about her pleasant experience with Addison-Wesley. Without her encouragement, I never would have started.

Most of what I know I've argued about with Tod Golding over the last nine years. Tod and I agree more often than either of us knows, but I always learn something from our arguments. I am indebted to Tod for all he's taught me over the years. Much of this book has been greatly enriched because of my conversations with him.

Thanks to Alex Viggio and everyone at XP Denver where I was able to present an early version of many of the ideas in this book. Thank you, also, to Mark Mosholder and J. B. Rainsberger, who talked to me about how they use software instead of note cards. Thank you to Kenny Rubin, co-author of *Succeeding With Objects* with Adele Goldberg, whose obvious pride in their book helped me want to write again after a few years off.

A hearty thank you to Mark and Dan Gutrich, the founders of Fast401k, who have wholeheartedly embraced user stories and Scrum. Thank you as well to each of my coworkers at Fast401k, where we are well on our way to achieving our goal of being one of the best teams in Colorado.

There is no way to thank my family enough for all the time they did without me. Thank you to my wonderful daughters and princesses, Savannah and Delaney. A special thank you to my wonderful and beautiful wife, Laura, for doing so much even when I do so little.

I owe a huge debt of gratitude to the team at Addison-Wesley. Paul Petralia made the process enjoyable from start to finish. Michele Vincenti kept things moving. Lisa Iarkowski offered me invaluable FrameMaker help. Gail Cocker made my illustrations worth looking at. And Nick Radhuber brought it all together at the end.

And last, but far from least, thank you to Kent Beck for his wonderful insights, his time, and for including this book in his Signature Series.

Introduction

I felt guilty throughout much of the mid-1990s. I was working for a company that was acquiring about one new company each year. Every time we'd buy a new company I would be assigned to run their software development group. And each of the acquired development groups came with glorious, beautiful, lengthy requirements documents. I inevitably felt guilty that my own groups were not producing such beautiful requirements specifications. Yet, my groups were consistently far more successful *at producing software* than were the groups we were acquiring.

I knew that what we were doing worked. Yet I had this nagging feeling that if we'd write big, lengthy requirements documents we could be even more successful. After all, that was what was being written in the books and articles I was reading at the time. If the successful software development teams were writing glorious requirements documents then it seemed like we should do the same. But, we never had the time. Our projects were always too important and were needed too soon for us to delay them at the start.

Because we never had the time to write a beautiful, lengthy requirements document, we settled on a way of working in which we would talk with our users. Rather than writing things down, passing them back and forth, and negotiating while the clock ran out, we talked. We'd draw screen samples on paper, sometimes we'd prototype, often we'd code a little and then show the intended users what we'd coded. At least once a month we'd grab a representative set of users and show them exactly what had been coded. By staying close to our users and by showing them progress in small pieces, we had found a way to be successful without the beautiful requirements documents.

Still, I felt guilty that we weren't doing things the way I thought we were supposed to.

In 1999 Kent Beck's revolutionary little book, *Extreme Programming Explained: Embrace Change,* was released. Overnight all of my guilt went away. Here was someone saying it was OK for developers and customers to talk rather than write, negotiate, and then write some more. Kent clarified a lot of things and gave me many new ways of working. But, most importantly, he justified what I'd learned from my own experience.

Extensive upfront requirements gathering and documentation can kill a project in many ways. One of the most common is when the requirements document itself becomes a goal. A requirements document should be written only when it helps achieve the real goal of delivering some software.

A second way that extensive upfront requirements gathering and documentation can kill a project is through the inaccuracies of written language. I remember many years ago being told a story about a child at bath time. The child's father has filled the bath tub and is helping his child into the water. The young child, probably two or three years old, dips a toe in the water, quickly removes it, and tells her father "make it warmer." The father puts his hand into the water and is surprised to find that, rather than too cold, the water is already warmer than what his daughter is used to.

After thinking about his child's request for a moment, the father realizes they are miscommunicating and are using the same words to mean different things. The child's request to "make it warmer" is interpreted by any adult to be the same as "increase the temperature." To the child, however, "make it warmer" meant "make it closer to the temperature I call warm."

Words, especially when written, are a very thin medium through which to express requirements for something as complex as software. With their ability to be misinterpreted we need to replace written words with frequent conversations between developers, customers, and users. User stories provide us with a way of having just enough written down that we don't forget and that we can estimate and plan while also encouraging this time of communication.

By the time you've finished the first part of this book you will be ready to begin the shift away from rigorously writing down every last requirement detail. By the time you've finished the book you will know everything necessary to implement a story-driven process in your environment. This book is organized in four parts and two appendices.

- Part I: Getting Started—A description of everything you need to know to get started writing stories *today*. One of the goals of user stories is to get people talking rather than writing. It is the goal of Part I to get you talking as soon as possible. The first chapter provides an overview of what a user story is and how you'll use stories. The next chapters in Part I provide additional detail on writing user stories, gathering stories through user role modeling, writing stories when you don't have access to real end users, and testing user stories. Part I concludes with a chapter providing guidelines that will improve your user stories.

- Part II: Estimating and Planning—Equipped with a collection of user stories, one of the first things we often need to answer is "How long will it take to develop?" The chapters of Part II cover how to estimate stories in story points, how to plan a release over a three- to six-month time horizon, how to plan an ensuing iteration in more detail, and, finally, how to measure progress and assess whether the project is progressing as you'd like.

- Part III: Frequently Discussed Topics—Part III starts by describing how stories differ from requirements alternatives such as use cases, software requirements specifications, and interaction design scenarios. The next chapters in Part III look at the unique advantages of user stories, how to tell when something is going wrong, and how to adapt the agile process Scrum to use stories. The final chapter of Part III looks at a variety of smaller issues such as whether to writes stories on paper note cards or in a software system and how to handle nonfunctional requirements.

- Part IV: An Example—An extended example intended to help bring everything together. If we're to make the claim that developers can best understand user's needs through stories then it is important to conclude this book with an extended story showing all aspects of user stories brought together in one example.

- Part V: Appendices—User stories originate in Extreme Programming. You do not need to be familiar with Extreme Programming in order to read this book. However, a brief introduction to Extreme Programming is provided in Appendix A. Appendix B contains answers to the questions that conclude the chapters.

PART I

Getting Started

In Part I, we start with a quick tour of what user stories are and how they're used. Following that we will look in more detail at how to write user stories, how to use the system's user types to help identify stories, how to work with people who may fill the user role when users themselves are hard to come by, and how to write tests that are used to know when a story has been successfully coded. After all that, we'll close Part I by looking at some guidelines for good stories.

When you're done with this section you'll know enough to get started with identifying, writing, and testing your own stories. You'll also be ready to look at how to estimate and plan with user stories, which will be the topic of Part II.

Chapter 1

An Overview

Software requirements is a communication problem. Those who want the new software (either to use or to sell) must communicate with those who will build the new software. To succeed, a project relies on information from the heads of very different people: on one side are customers and users and sometimes analysts, domain experts and others who view the software from a business or organizational perspective; on the other side is the technical team.

If either side dominates these communications, the project loses. When the business side dominates, it mandates functionality and dates with little concern that the developers can meet both objectives, or whether the developers understand exactly what is needed. When the developers dominate the communications, technical jargon replaces the language of the business and the developers lose the opportunity to learn what is needed by listening.

What we need is a way to work together so that neither side dominates and so that the emotionally-fraught and political issue of resource allocation becomes a shared problem. Projects fail when the problem of resource allocation falls entirely on one side. If the developers shoulder the problem (usually in the form of being told "I don't care how you do it but do it all by June") they may trade quality for additional features, may only partially implement a feature, or may solely make any of a number of decisions in which the customers and users should participate. When customers and users shoulder the burden of resource allocation, we usually see a lengthy series of discussions at the start of a project during which features are progressively removed from the project. Then, when the software is eventually delivered, it has even less functionality than the reduced set that was identified.

By now we've learned that we cannot perfectly predict a software development project. As users see early versions of the software, they come up with new ideas and their opinions change. Because of the intangibility of software, most developers have a notoriously difficult time estimating how long things will take. Because of these and other factors we cannot lay out a perfect PERT chart showing everything that must be done on a project.

So, what do we do?

We make decisions based on the information we have at hand. And we do it often. Rather than making one all-encompassing set of decisions at the outset of a project, we spread the decision-making across the duration of the project. To do this we make sure we have a process that gets us information as early and often as possible. And this is where user stories come in.

What Is a User Story?

A user story describes functionality that will be valuable to either a user or purchaser of a system or software. User stories are composed of three aspects:

- a written description of the story used for planning and as a reminder

- conversations about the story that serve to flesh out the details of the story

- tests that convey and document details and that can be used to determine when a story is complete

Because user story descriptions are traditionally hand-written on paper note cards, Ron Jeffries has named these three aspects with the wonderful alliteration of Card, Conversation, and Confirmation (Jeffries 2001). The Card may be the most visible manifestation of a user story, but it is not the most important. Rachel Davies (2001) has said that cards "*represent* customer requirements rather than *document* them." This is the perfect way to think about user stories: While the card may contain the text of the story, the details are worked out in the Conversation and recorded in the Confirmation.

As an example user story see Story Card 1.1, which is a story card from the hypothetical BigMoneyJobs job posting and search website.

A user can post her resume to the website.

■ Story Card 1.1   An initial user story written on a note card.

For consistency, many of the examples throughout the rest of this book will be for the BigMoneyJobs website. Other sample stories for BigMoneyJobs might include:

- A user can search for jobs.

- A company can post new job openings.

- A user can limit who can see her resume.

Because user stories represent functionality that will be valued by users, the following examples do not make good user stories for this system:

- The software will be written in C++.

- The program will connect to the database through a connection pool.

The first example is not a good user story for BigMoneyJobs because its users would not care which programming language was used. However, if this were an application programming interface, then the user of that system (herself a programmer) could very well have written that "the software will be written in C++."

The second story is not a good user story in this case because the users of this system do not care about the technical details of how the application connects to the database.

Perhaps you've read these stories and are screaming "But wait— using a connection pool is a requirement in my system!" If so, hold on, the key is that stories should be written so that the customer can value them. There are ways to express stories like these in ways that are valuable to a customer. We'll see examples of doing that in Chapter 2, "Writing Stories."

Where Are the Details?

It's one thing to say "A user can search for jobs." It's another thing to be able to start coding and testing with only that as guidance. Where are the details? What about all the unanswered questions like:

- What values can users search on? State? City? Job title? Keywords?

- Does the user have to be a member of the site?

- Can search parameters be saved?

- What information is displayed for matching jobs?

Many of these details can be expressed as additional stories. In fact, it is better to have more stories than to have stories that are too large. For example, the entire BigMoneyJobs site is probably described by these two stories:

- A user can search for a job.

- A company can post job openings.

Clearly these two stories are too large to be of much use. Chapter 2, "Writing Stories," fully addresses the question of story size, but as a starting point it's good to have stories that can be coded and tested between half a day and perhaps two weeks by one or a pair of programmers. Liberally interpreted, the two stories above could easily cover the majority of the BigMoneyJobs site so each will likely take most programmers more than a week.

When a story is too large it is sometimes referred to as an *epic*. Epics can be split into two or more stories of smaller size. For example, the epic "A user can search for a job" could be split into these stories:

- A user can search for jobs by attributes like location, salary range, job title, company name, and the date the job was posted.

- A user can view information about each job that is matched by a search.

- A user can view detailed information about a company that has posted a job.

However, we do not continue splitting stories until we have a story that covers every last detail. For example, the story "A user can view information about each job that is matched by a search" is a very reasonable and realistic story. We do not need to further divide it into:

- A user can view a job description.

- A user can view a job's salary range.

- A user can view the location of a job.

Similarly, the user story does not need to be augmented in typical requirements documentation style like this:

4.6)   A user can view information about each job that is matched
         by a search.
    4.6.1)   A user can view the job description.
    4.6.2)   A user can view a job's salary range.
    4.6.3)   A user can view the location of a job.

Rather than writing all these details as stories, the better approach is for the development team and the customer to discuss these details. That is, have a conversation about the details at the point when the details become important. There's nothing wrong with making a few annotations on a story card based on a discussion, as shown in Story Card 1.2. However, the conversation is the key, not the note on the story card. Neither the developers nor the customer can point to the card three months later and say, "But, see I said so right there." Stories are not contractual obligations. As we'll see, agreements are documented by tests that demonstrate that a story has been developed correctly.

> Users can view information about each job that is matched by a search.
>
>
> Marco says show description, salary, and location.

■ Story Card 1.2   A story card with a note.

"How Long Does It Have to Be?"

I was the kid in high school literature classes who always asked, "How long does it have to be?" whenever we were assigned to write a paper. The teachers never liked the question but I still think it was a fair one because it told me what their expectations were. It is just as important to understand the expectations of a project's users. Those expectations are best captured in the form of the acceptance tests.

If you're using paper note cards, you can turn the card over and capture these expectations there. The expectations are written as reminders about how to test the story as shown in Story Card 1.3. If you're using an electronic system it probably has a place you can enter the acceptance test reminders.

> Try it with an empty job description.
> Try it with a really long job description.
> Try it with a missing salary.
> Try it with a six-digit salary.

■ Story Card 1.3   The back of a story card holds reminders about how to test the story.

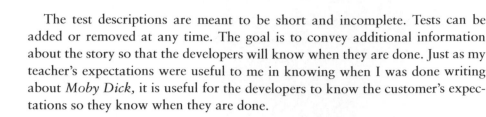

The test descriptions are meant to be short and incomplete. Tests can be added or removed at any time. The goal is to convey additional information about the story so that the developers will know when they are done. Just as my teacher's expectations were useful to me in knowing when I was done writing about *Moby Dick,* it is useful for the developers to know the customer's expectations so they know when they are done.

The Customer Team

On an ideal project we would have a single person who prioritizes work for developers, omnisciently answers their questions, will use the software when it's finished, and writes all of the stories. This is almost always too much to hope for, so we establish a customer team. The customer team includes those who ensure that the software will meet the needs of its intended users. This means the customer team may include testers, a product manager, real users, and interaction designers.

What Will the Process Be Like?

A project that is using stories will have a different feel and rhythm than you may be used to. Using a traditional waterfall-oriented process leads to a cycle of write all the requirements, analyze the requirements, design a solution, code the solution, and then finally test it. Very often during this type of process, customers and users are involved at the beginning to write requirements and at the end to accept the software, but user and customer involvement may almost entirely disappear between requirements and acceptance. By now, we've learned that this doesn't work.

The first thing you'll notice on a story-driven project is that customers and users remain involved throughout the duration of the project. They are not expected (or allowed!) to disappear during the middle of the project. This is true whether the team will be using Extreme Programming (XP; see Appendix A, "An Overview of Extreme Programming," for more information), an agile version of the Unified Process, an agile process like Scrum (see Chapter 15, "Using Stories with Scrum"), or a home-grown, story-driven agile process.

The customers and intended users of the new software should plan on taking a very active role in writing the user stories, especially if using XP. The story writing process is best started by considering the types of users of the intended system. For example, if you are building a travel reservation website, you may have user types such as frequent fliers, vacation planners, and so on. The customer team should include representatives of as many of these user types as practical. But when it can't, user role modeling can help. (For more on this topic see Chapter 3, "User Role Modeling.")

Why Does the Customer Write the Stories?

The customer team, rather than the developers, writes the user stories for two primary reasons. First, each story must be written in the language of the business, not in technical jargon, so that the customer team can prioritize the stories for inclusion into iterations and releases. Second, as the primary product visionaries, the customer team is in the best position to describe the behavior of the product.

A project's initial stories are often written in a story writing workshop, but stories can be written at any time throughout the project. During the story writing workshop, everyone brainstorms as many stories as possible. Armed with a starting set of stories, the developers estimate the size of each.

Collaboratively, the customer team and developers select an iteration length, from perhaps one to four weeks. The same iteration length will be used for the duration of the project. By the end of each iteration the developers will be responsible for delivering fully usable code for some subset of the application. The customer team remains highly involved during the iteration, talking with the developers about the stories being developed during that iteration. During the iteration the customer team also specifies tests and works with the developers to automate and run tests. Additionally, the customer team makes sure the project is constantly moving toward delivery of the desired product.

Once an iteration length has been selected, the developers will estimate how much work they'll be able to do per iteration. We call this *velocity*. The team's first estimate of velocity will be wrong because there's no way to know velocity in advance. However, we can use the initial estimate to make a rough sketch, or release plan, of what work will happen in each iteration and how many iterations will be needed.

To plan a release, we sort stories into various piles with each pile representing an iteration. Each pile will contain some number of stories, the estimates for which add up to no more than the estimated velocity. The highest-priority stories go into the first pile. When that pile is full, the next highest-priority stories go into a second pile (representing the second iteration). This continues until you've either made so many piles that you're out of time for the project or until the piles represent a desirable new release of the product. (For more on these topics see Chapter 9, "Planning a Release," and Chapter 10, "Planning an Iteration.")

Prior to the start of each iteration the customer team can make mid-course corrections to the plan. As iterations are completed, we learn the development team's actual velocity and can work with it instead of the estimated velocity. This means that each pile of stories may need to be adjusted by adding or removing stories. Also, some stories will turn out to be far easier than anticipated, which means the team will sometimes want to be given an additional story to do in that iteration. But some stories will be harder than anticipated, which means that some work will need to be moved into later iterations or out of the release altogether.

Planning Releases and Iterations

A release is made up of one or more iterations. Release planning refers to determining a balance between a projected timeline and a desired set of functionality. Iteration planning refers to selecting stories for inclusion in this iteration. The customer team and the developers are both involved in release and iteration planning.

To plan a release, the customer team starts by prioritizing the stories. While prioritizing they will want to consider:

- The desirability of the feature to a broad base of users or customers

- The desirability of the feature to a small number of important users or customers

- The cohesiveness of the story in relation to other stories. For example, a "zoom out" story may not be high priority on its own but may be treated as such because it is complementary to "zoom in," which is high priority.

The developers have different priorities for many of the stories. They may suggest that the priority of a story be changed based on its technical risk or because it is complementary to another story. The customer team listens to their opinions but then prioritizes stories in the manner that maximizes the value delivered to the organization.

Stories cannot be prioritized without considering their costs. My priority for a vacation spot last summer was Tahiti until I considered its cost. At that point other locations moved up in priority. Factored into the prioritization is the cost of each story. The cost of a story is the estimate given to it by the developers. Each story is assigned an estimate in *story points*, which indicates the size and complexity of the story relative to other stories. So, a story estimated at four story points is expected to take twice as long as a story estimated at two story points.

The release plan is built by assigning stories to the iterations in the release. The developers state their expected velocity, which is the number of story points they think they will complete per iteration. The customer then allocates stories to iterations, making sure that the number of story points assigned to any one iteration does not exceed the expected team velocity.

As an example, suppose that Table 1.1 lists all the stories in your project and they are sorted in order of descending priority. The team estimates a velocity of thirteen story points per iteration. Stories would be allocated to iterations as shown in Table 1.2.

Table 1.1 *Sample stories and their costs.*

Story	Story Points
Story A	3
Story B	5
Story C	5
Story D	3
Story E	1
Story F	8
Story G	5
Story H	5
Story I	5
Story J	2

Because the team expects a velocity of thirteen, no iteration can be planned to have more than thirteen story points in it. This means that the second and third iterations are planned to have only twelve story points. Don't worry about it—estimation is rarely precise enough for this difference to matter, and if the developers go faster than planned they'll ask for another small story or two. Notice that for the third iteration the customer team has actually chosen to include Story J over the higher priority Story I. This is because Story I, at five story points, is actually too large to include in the third iteration.

Table 1.2 *A release plan for the stories of Table 1.1.*

Iteration	Stories	Story Points
Iteration 1	A, B, C	13
Iteration 2	D, E, F	12
Iteration 3	G, H, J	12
Iteration 4	I	5

An alternative to temporarily skipping a large story and putting a smaller one in its place in an iteration is to split the large story into two stories. Suppose that the five-point Story I could have been split into Story Y (three points) and Story Z (two points). Story Y contains the most important parts of the old Story I and can now fit in the third iteration, as shown in Table 1.3. For advice on how and when to split stories see Chapter 2, "Writing Stories," and Chapter 7, "Guidelines for Good Stories."

Table 1.3 *Splitting a story to create a better release plan.*

Iteration	Stories	Story Points
Iteration 1	A, B, C	13
Iteration 2	D, E, F	12
Iteration 3	G, H, Y	13
Iteration 4	J, Z	4

What Are Acceptance Tests?

Acceptance testing is the process of verifying that stories were developed such that each works exactly the way the customer team expected it to work. Once an iteration begins, the developers start coding and the customer team starts specifying tests. Depending on the technical proficiency of customer team members, this may mean anything from writing tests on the back of the story card to putting the tests into an automated testing tool. A dedicated and skilled tester should be included on the customer team for the more technical of these tasks.

Tests should be written as early in an iteration as possible (or even slightly before the iteration if you're comfortable taking a slight guess at what will be in the upcoming iteration). Writing tests early is extremely helpful because more of the customer team's assumptions and expectations are communicated earlier to the developers. For example, suppose you write the story "A user can pay for the items in her shopping cart with a credit card." You then write these simple tests on the back of that story card:

- Test with Visa, MasterCard and American Express (pass).

- Test with Diner's Club (fail).

- Test with a Visa debit card (pass).

- Test with good, bad and missing card ID numbers from the back of the card.

- Test with expired cards.

- Test with different purchase amounts (including one over the card's limit).

These tests capture the expectations that the system will handle Visa, MasterCard and American Express and will not allow purchases with other cards. By giving these tests to the programmer early, the customer team has not only stated their expectations, they may also have reminded the programmer of a situation she had otherwise forgotten. For example, she may have forgotten to consider expired cards. Noting it as a test on the back of the card before she starts programming will save her time. For more on writing acceptance tests for stories see Chapter 6, "Acceptance Testing User Stories."

Why Change?

At this point you may be asking why change? Why write story cards and hold all these conversatons? Why not just continue to write requirements documents or use cases? User stories offer a number of advantages over alternative approaches. More details are provided in Chapter 13, "Why User Stories?", but some of the reasons are:

- User stories emphasize verbal rather than written communication.

- User stories are comprehensible by both you and the developers.

- User stories are the right size for planning.

- User stories work for iterative development.

• User stories encourage deferring detail until you have the best understanding you are going to have about what you really need.

Because user stories shift emphasis toward talking and away from writing, important decisions are not captured in documents that are unlikely to be read. Instead, important aspects about stories are captured in automated acceptance tests and run frequently. Additionally, we avoid obtuse written documents with statements like:

> The system must store an address and business phone number or mobile phone number.

What does that mean? It could mean that the system must store one of these:

> (Address and business phone) or mobile phone
> Address and (business phone or mobile phone)

Because user stories are free of technical jargon (remember, the customer team writes them), they are comprehensible by both the developers as well as the customer team.

Each user story represents a discrete piece of functionality; that is, something a user would be likely to do in a single setting. This makes user stories appropriate as a planning tool. You can assess the value of shifting stories between releases far better than you can assess the impact of leaving out one or more "The system shall…" statements.

An iterative process is one that makes progress through successive refinement. A development team takes a first cut at a system, knowing it is incomplete or weak in some (perhaps many) areas. They then successively refine those areas until the product is satisfactory. With each iteration the software is improved through the addition of greater detail. Stories work well for iterative development because it is also possible to iterate over the stories. For a feature that you want eventually but that isn't important right now, you can first write a large story (an epic). When you're ready to add that story into the system you can refine it by ripping up the epic and replacing it with smaller stories that will be easier to work with.

It is this ability to iterate over a story set that allows stories to encourage the deferring of detail. Because we can write a placeholder epic today, there is no need to write stories about parts of a system until close to when those parts will be developed. Deferring detail is important because it allows us to not spend time thinking about a new feature until we are positive the feature is needed. Stories discourage us from pretending we can know and write everything in advance. Instead they encourage a process whereby software is iteratively refined based on discussions between the customer team and the developers.

Summary

- A story card contains a short description of user- or customer-valued functionality.

- A story card is the visible part of a story, but the important parts are the conversations between the customer and developers about the story.

- The customer team includes those who ensure that the software will meet the needs of its intended users. This may include testers, a product manager, real users, and interaction designers.

- The customer team writes the story cards because they are in the best position to express the desired features and because they must later be able to work out story details with the developers and to prioritize the stories.

- Stories are prioritized based on their value to the organization.

- Releases and iterations are planned by placing stories into iterations.

- Velocity is the amount of work the developers can complete in an iteration.

- The sum of the estimates of the stories placed in an iteration cannot exceed the velocity the developers forecast for that iteration.

- If a story won't fit in an iteration, you can split the story into two or more smaller stories.

- Acceptance tests validate that a story has been developed with the functionality the customer team had in mind when they wrote the story.

- User stories are worth using because they emphasize verbal communication, can be understood equally by you and the developers, can be used for planning iterations, work well within an iterative development process, and because they encourage the deferring of detail.

Questions

1.1   What are the three parts of a user story?

1.2   Who is on the customer team?

1.3   Which of the following are not good stories? Why?

a The user can run the system on Windows XP and Linux.

b All graphing and charting will be done using a third-party library.

c The user can undo up to fifty commands.

d The software will be released by June 30.

e The software will be written in Java.

f The user can select her country from a drop-down list.

g The system will use Log4J to log all error messages to a file.

h The user will be prompted to save her work if she hasn't saved it for 15 minutes.

i The user can select an "Export to XML" feature.

j The user can export data to XML.

1.4 What advantages do requirements conversations have over requirements documents?

1.5 Why would you want to write tests on the back of a story card?

Chapter 2

Writing Stories

In this chapter we turn our attention to writing the stories. To create good stories we focus on six attributes. A good story is:

- Independent

- Negotiable

- Valuable to users or customers

- Estimatable

- Small

- Testable

Bill Wake, author of *Extreme Programming Explored* and *Refactoring Workbook*, has suggested the acronym INVEST for these six attributes (Wake 2003a).

Independent

As much as possible, care should be taken to avoid introducing dependencies between stories. Dependencies between stories lead to prioritization and planning problems. For example, suppose the customer has selected as high priority a story that is dependent on a story that is low priority. Dependencies between stories can also make estimation much harder than it needs to be. For example, suppose we are working on the BigMoneyJobs website and need to write stories for how companies can pay for the job openings they post to our site. We could write these stories:

1. A company can pay for a job posting with a Visa card.

2. A company can pay for a job posting with a MasterCard.

3.   A company can pay for a job posting with an American Express card.

Suppose the developers estimate that it will take three days to support the first credit card type (regardless of which it is) and then one day each for the second and third. With highly dependent stories such as these you don't know what estimate to give each story—which story should be given the three day estimate?

When presented with this type of dependency, there are two ways around it:

- Combine the dependent stories into one larger but independent story

- Find a different way of splitting the stories

Combining the stories about the different credit card types into a single large story ("A company can pay for a job posting with a credit card") works well in this case because the combined story is only five days long. If the combined story is much longer than that, a better approach is usually to find a different dimension along which to split the stories. If the estimates for these stories had been longer, then an alternative split would be:

1.   A customer can pay with one type of credit card.

2.   A customer can pay with two additional types of credit cards.

If you don't want to combine the stories and can't find a good way to split them, you can always take the simple approach of putting two estimates on the card: one estimate if the story is done before the other story, a lower estimate if it is done after.

Negotiable

Stories are negotiable. They are not written contracts or requirements that the software must implement. Story cards are short descriptions of functionality, the details of which are to be negotiated in a conversation between the customer and the development team. Because story cards are reminders to have a conversation rather than fully detailed requirements themselves, they do not need to include all relevant details. However, if at the time the story is written some important details are known, they should be included as annotations to the story card, as shown in Story Card 2.1. The challenge comes in learning to include just enough detail.

Story Card 2.1 works well because it provides the right amount of information to the developer and customer who will talk about the story. When a devel-

A company can pay for a job posting with a credit card.

Note: Accept Visa, MasterCard, and American Express.
Consider Discover.

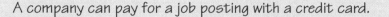

■   Story Card 2.1   A story card with notes providing additional detail.

oper starts to code this story, she will be reminded that a decision has already
been made to accept the three main cards and she can ask the customer if a
decision has been made about accepting Discover cards. The notes on the card
help a developer and the customer to resume a conversation where it left off
previously. Ideally, the conversation can be resumed this easily regardless of
whether it is the same developer and customer who resume the conversation.
Use this as a guideline when adding detail to stories.

On the other hand, consider a story that is annotated with too many notes,
as shown in Story Card 2.2. This story has too much detail ("Collect the expiration month and date of the card") and also combines what should probably
be a separate story ("The system can store a card number for future use").

A company can pay for a job posting with a credit card.
Note: Accept Visa, MasterCard, and American Express.
Consider Discover. On purchases over $100, ask for card ID
number from back of card. The system can tell what type of card
it is from the first two digits of the card number. The system
can store a card number for future use. Collect the expiration
month and date of the card.

■   Story Card 2.2   A story card with too much detail.

Working with stories like Story Card 2.2 is very difficult. Most readers of
this type of story will mistakenly associate the extra detail with extra precision.
However, in many cases specifying details too soon just creates more work. For
example, if two developers discuss and estimate a story that says simply "a
company can pay for a job posting with a credit card" they will not forget that
their discussion is somewhat abstract. There are too many missing details for

them to mistakenly view their discussion as definitive or their estimate as accurate. However, when as much detail is added as in Story Card 2.2, discussions about the story are much more likely to feel concrete and real. This can lead to the mistaken belief that the story cards reflect all the details and that there's no further need to discuss the story with the customer.

If we think about the story card as a reminder for the developer and customer to have a conversation, then it is useful to think of the story card as containing:

- a phrase or two that act as reminders to hold the conversation

- notes about issues to be resolved during the conversation

Details that have already been determined through conversations become tests. Tests can be noted on the back of the story card if using note cards or in whatever electronic system is being used. Story Card 2.3 and Story Card 2.4 show how the excess detail of Story Card 2.2 can be turned into tests, leaving just notes for the conversation as part of the front of the story card. In this way, the front of a story card contains the story and notes about open questions while the back of the card contains details about the story in the form of tests that will prove whether or not it works as expected.

A company can pay for a job posting with a credit card.

Note: Will we accept Discover cards?
Note for UI: Don't have a field for card type (it can be derived from first two digits on the card).

■ Story Card 2.3   The revised front of a story card with only the story and questions to be discussed.

Valuable to Purchasers or Users

It is tempting to say something along the lines of "Each story must be valued by the users." But that would be wrong. Many projects include stories that are not valued by users. Keeping in mind the distinction between *user* (someone who uses the software) and *purchaser* (someone who purchases the software), suppose a development team is building software that will be deployed across a

> Test with Visa, MasterCard and American Express (pass).
> Test with Diner's Club (fail).
> Test with good, bad and missing card ID numbers.
> Test with expired cards.
> Test with over $100 and under $100.

■ Story Card 2.4   Details that imply test cases are separated from the story itself. Here they are shown on the back of the story card.

large user base, perhaps 5,000 computers in a single company. The purchaser of a product like that may be very concerned that each of the 5,000 computers is using the same configuration for the software. This may lead to a story like "All configuration information is read from a central location." Users don't care where configuration information is stored but purchasers might.

Similarly, stories like the following might be valued by purchasers contemplating buying the product but would not be valued by actual users:

- Throughout the development process, the development team will produce documentation suitable for an ISO 9001 audit.

- The development team will produce the software in accordance with CMM Level 3.

What you want to avoid are stories that are only valued by developers. For example, avoid stories like these:

- All connections to the database are through a connection pool.

- All error handling and logging is done through a set of common classes.

As written, these stories are focused on the technology and the advantages to the programmers. It is very possible that the ideas behind these stories are good ones but they should instead be written so that the benefits to the customers or the user are apparent. This will allow the customer to intelligently prioritize these stories into the development schedule. Better variations of these stories could be the following:

- Up to fifty users should be able to use the application with a five-user database license.

- All errors are presented to the user and logged in a consistent manner.

In exactly the same way it is worth attempting to keep user interface assumptions out of stories, it is also worth keeping technology assumptions out of stories. For example, the revised stories above have removed the implicit use of a connection pool and a set of error handling classes.

The best way to ensure that each story is valuable to the customer or users is to have the customer write the stories. Customers are often uncomfortable with this initially—probably because developers have trained them to think of everything they write as something that can be held against them later. ("Well, the requirements document didn't say that...") Most customers begin writing stories themselves once they become comfortable with the concept that story cards are reminders to talk later rather than formal commitments or descriptions of specific functionality.

Estimatable

It is important for developers to be able to estimate (or at least take a guess at) the size of a story or the amount of time it will take to turn a story into working code. There are three common reasons why a story may not be estimatable:

1.   Developers lack domain knowledge.

2.   Developers lack technical knowledge.

3.   The story is too big.

First, the developers may lack domain knowledge. If the developers do not understand a story as it is written, they should discuss it with the customer who wrote the story. Again, it's not necessary to understand all the details about a story, but the developers need to have a general understanding of the story.

Second, a story may not be estimatable because the developers do not understand the technology involved. For example, on one Java project we were asked to provide a CORBA interface into the system. No one on the team had done that so there was no way to estimate the task. The solution in this case is to send one or more developers on what Extreme Programming calls a *spike*, which is a brief experiment to learn about an area of the application. During the spike the developers learn just enough that they can estimate the task. The spike itself is always given a defined maximum amount of time (called a *timebox*), which allows us to estimate the spike. In this way an unestimatable story turns into two stories: a quick spike to gather information and then a story to do the real work.

Finally, the developers may not be able to estimate a story if it is too big. For example, for the BigMoneyJobs website, the story "A Job Seeker can find a job" is too large. In order to estimate it the developers will need to disaggregate it into smaller, constituent stories.

A Lack of Domain Knowledge

As an example of needing more domain knowledge, we were building a website for long-term medical care of chronic conditions. The customer (a highly qualified nurse) wrote a story saying "New users are given a diabetic screening." The developers weren't sure what that meant and it could have run the gamut from a simple web questionnaire to actually sending something to new users for an at-home physical screening, as was done for the company's product for asthma patients. The developers got together with the customer and found out that she was thinking of a simple web form with a handful of questions.

Even though they are too big to estimate reliably, it is sometimes useful to write epics such as "A Job Seeker can find a job" because they serve as place-holders or reminders about big parts of a system that need to be discussed. If you are making a conscious decision to temporarily gloss over large parts of a system, then consider writing an epic or two that cover those parts. The epic can be assigned a large, pulled–from–thin–air estimate.

Small

Like Goldilocks in search of a comfortable bed, some stories can be too big, some can be too small, and some can be just right. Story size does matter because if stories are too large or too small you cannot use them in planning. Epics are difficult to work with because they frequently contain multiple stories. For example, in a travel reservation system, "A user can plan a vacation" is an epic. Planning a vacation is important functionality for a travel reservation system but there are many tasks involved in doing so. The epic should be split into smaller stories. The ultimate determination of whether a story is appropriately sized is based on the team, its capabilities, and the technologies in use.

Splitting Stories

Epics typically fall into one of two categories:

- The compound story

- The complex story

A compound story is an epic that comprises multiple shorter stories. For example, the BigMoneyJobs system may include the story "A user can post her resume." During the initial planning of the system this story may be appropriate. But when the developers talk to the customer, they find out that "post her resume" actually means:

- that a resume can include education, prior jobs, salary history, publications, presentations, community service, and an objective

- that users can mark resumes as inactive

- that users can have multiple resumes

- that users can edit resumes

- that users can delete resumes

Depending on how long these will take to develop, each could become its own unique story. However, that may just take an epic and go too far in the opposite direction, turning it into a series of stories that are too small. For example, depending on the technologies in use and the size and skill of the team, stories like these will generally be too small:

- A Job Seeker can enter a date for each community service entry on a resume.

- A Job Seeker can edit the date for each community service entry on a resume.

- A Job Seeker can enter a date range for each prior job on a resume.

- A Job Seeker can edit the date range for each prior job on a resume.

Generally, a better solution is to group the smaller stories as follows:

- A user can create resumes, which include education, prior jobs, salary history, publications, presentations, community service, and an objective.

- A user can edit a resume.

- A user can delete a resume.

- A user can have multiple resumes.

- A user can activate and inactivate resumes.

There are normally many ways to disaggregate a compound story. The preceding disaggregation is along the lines of create, edit, and delete, which is commonly used. This works well if the create story is small enough that it can be left as one story. An alternative is to disaggregate along the boundaries of the data. To do this, think of each component of a resume as being added and edited individually. This leads to a completely different disaggregation:

- A user can add and edit education information.

- A user can add and edit job history information.

- A user can add and edit salary history information.

- A user can add and edit publications.

- A user can add and edit presentations.

- A user can add and edit community service.

- A user can add and edit an objective.

And so on.

Unlike the compound story, the complex story is a user story that is inherently large and cannot easily be disaggregated into a set of constituent stories. If a story is complex because of uncertainty associated with it, you may want to split the story into two stories: one investigative and one developing the new feature. For example, suppose the developers are given the story "A company can pay for a job posting with a credit card" but none of the developers has ever done credit card processing before. They may choose to split the stories like this:

- Investigate credit card processing over the web.

- A user can pay with a credit card.

In this case the first story will send one or more developers on a spike. When complex stories are split in this way, always define a timebox around the investigative story, or spike. Even if the story cannot be estimated with any reasonable accuracy, it is still possible to define the maximum amount of time that will be spent learning.

Complex stories are also common when developing new or extending known algorithms. One team in a biotech company had a story to add novel extensions to a standard statistical approach called expectation maximization. The complex story was rewritten as two stories: the first to research and determine the feasibility of extending expectation maximization; the second to add that functionality to the product. In situations like this one it is difficult to estimate how long the research story will take.

Consider Putting the Spike in a Different Iteration

When possible, it works well to put the investigative story in one iteration and the other stories in one or more subsequent iterations. Normally, only the investigative story can be estimated. Including the other, non-estimatable stories in the same iteration with the investigative story means there will be a higher than normal level of uncertainty about how much can be accomplished in that iteration.

The key benefit of breaking out a story that cannot be estimated is that it allows the customer to prioritize the research separately from the new functionality. If the customer has only the complex story to prioritize ("Add novel extensions to standard expectation maximization") and an estimate for the story, she may prioritize the story based on the mistaken assumption that the new functionality will be delivered in approximately that timeframe. If instead, the customer has an investigative, spike story ("research and determine the feasibility of extending expectation maximization") and a functional story ("extend expectation maximization"), she must choose between adding the investigative story that adds no new functionality this iteration and perhaps some other story that does.

Combining Stories

Sometimes stories are too small. A story that is too small is typically one that the developer says she doesn't want to write down or estimate because doing that may take longer than making the change. Bug reports and user interface changes are common examples of stories that are often too small. A good approach for tiny stories, common among Extreme Programming teams, is to combine them into larger stories that represent from about a half-day to several days of work. The combined story is given a name and is then scheduled and worked on just like any other story.

For example, suppose a project has five bugs and a request to change some colors on the search screen. The developers estimate the total work involved and the entire collection is treated as a single story. If you've chosen to use paper note cards, you can do this by stapling them together with a cover card.

Testable

Stories must be written so as to be testable. Successfully passing its tests proves that a story has been successfully developed. If the story cannot be tested, how can the developers know when they have finished coding?

Untestable stories commonly show up for nonfunctional requirements, which are requirements about the software but not directly about its functionality. For example, consider these nonfunctional stories:

- A user must find the software easy to use.

- A user must never have to wait long for any screen to appear.

As written, these stories are not testable. Whenever possible, tests should be automated. This means strive for 99% automation, not 10%. You can almost always automate more than you think you can. When a product is developed incrementally, things can change very quickly and code that worked yesterday can stop working today. You want automated tests that will find this as soon as possible.

There is a very small subset of tests that cannot realistically be automated. For example, a user story that says "A novice user is able to complete common workflows without training" can be tested but cannot be automated. Testing this story will likely involve having a human factors expert design a test that involves observation of a random sample of representative novice users. That type of test can be both time-consuming and expensive, but the story is testable and may be appropriate for some products.

The story "a user never has to wait long for any screen to appear" is not testable because it says "never" and because it does not define what "wait long" means. Demonstrating that something never happens is impossible. A far easier, and more reasonable target, is to demonstrate that something rarely happens. This story could have instead been written as "New screens appear within two seconds in 95% of all cases." And—even better—an automated test can be written to verify this.

Summary

- Ideally, stories are independent from one another. This isn't always possible but to the extent it is, stories should be written so that they can be developed in any order.

- The details of a story are negotiated between the user and the developers.

- Stories should be written so that their value to users or the customer is clear. The best way to achieve this is to have the customer write the stories.

- Stories may be annotated with details, but too much detail obscures the meaning of the story and can give the impression that no conversation is necessary between the developers and the customer.

- One of the best ways to annotate a story is to write test cases for the story.

- If they are too big, compound and complex stories may be split into multiple smaller stories.

- If they are too small, multiple tiny stories may be combined into one bigger story.

- Stories need to be testable.

Developer Responsibilities

- You are responsible for helping the customer write stories that are promises to converse rather than detailed specifications, have value to users or the customer, are independent, are testable, and are appropriately sized.

- If tempted to ask for a story about the use of a technology or a piece of infrastructure, you are responsible for instead describing the need in terms of its value to users or the customer.

Customer Responsibilities

- You are responsible for writing stories that are promises to converse rather than detailed specifications, have value to users or to yourself, are independent, are testable, and are appropriately sized.

Questions

2.1   For the following stories, indicate if it is a good story or not. If not, why?

    a   A user can quickly master the system.

    b   A user can edit the address on a resume.

    c   A user can add, edit and delete multiple resumes.

    d   The system can calculate saddlepoint approximations for distributions of quadratic forms in normal variables.

    e   All runtime errors are logged in a consistent manner.

2.2   Break this epic up into appropriately sized component stories: "A user can make and change automated job search agents."

Chapter 3

User Role Modeling

On many projects, stories are written as though there is only one type of user. All stories are written from the perspective of that user type. This simplification is a fallacy and can lead a team to miss stories for users who do not fit the general mold of the system's primary user type. The disciplines of usage-centered design (Constantine and Lockwood 1999) and interaction design (Cooper 1999) teach us the benefits of identifying user roles and personas prior to writing stories. In this chapter we will look at user roles, role modeling, user role maps, and personas and show how taking these initial steps leads to better stories and better software.

User Roles[1]

Suppose we are building the BigMoneyJobs job posting and search site. This type of site will have many different types of users. When we talk about *user stories*, who is the user we're talking about? Are we talking about Ashish who has a job but always keeps an eye out for a better one? Are we talking about Laura, a new college graduate looking for her first professional job? Are we talking about Allan, who has decided he'll take any job that lets him move to Maui and windsurf every afternoon? Or are we talking about Scott, who doesn't hate his job but has realized it's time to move on? Perhaps we're talking about Kindra who was laid off six months ago and was looking for a great job but will now take anything in the northeastern United States.

Or should we think of the user as coming from one of the companies posting the jobs? Perhaps the user is Mario, who works in human resources and posts

---

1. Much of the discussion of user roles in this chapter is based on the work of Larry Constantine and Lucy Lockwood. Further information on user role modeling is available at their website at www.foruse.com or in *Software for Use* (1999).

new job openings. Perhaps the user is Delaney, who also works in human resources but is responsible for reviewing resumes. Or perhaps the user is Savannah, who works as an independent recruiter and is looking for both good jobs and good people.

Clearly we cannot write stories from a single perspective and have those stories reflect the experiences, backgrounds and goals of each of these users. Ashish, an accountant, may look at the site once a month just to keep his options open. Allan, a waiter, may want to create a filter to notify him any time any job on Maui gets posted but he won't be able to do that unless we make it easy. Kindra may spend hours each day looking for a job, broadening her search as time goes by. If Mario and Delaney work for a large company with many positions to fill, they may spend four or more hours a day on the site.

While each user comes to your software with a different background and with different goals, it is still possible to aggregate individual users and think of them in terms of *user roles*. A user role is a collection of defining attributes that characterize a population of users and their intended interactions with the system. So, we could look at the users in the preceding example and group them into roles as shown in Table 3.1 into roles this way.

Table 3.1 *One possible list of roles for the BigMoneyJobs project.*

Role	Who
Job Seeker	Scott
First Timer	Laura
Layoff Victim	Kindra
Geographic Searcher	Allan
Monitor	Ashish
Job Poster	Mario, Savannah
Resume Reader	Delaney, Savannah

Naturally, there will be some overlap between different user roles. The Job Seeker, First Timer, Layoff Victim, Geographic Searcher, and Monitor roles will all use the job search features of the site. They may use them in different ways and at different frequencies, but much of how they use the system will be similar. The Resume Reader and Job Poster roles will probably overlap as well since these roles are both pursuing the same goal of finding good candidates.

Table 3.1 does not show the only possible way to group users of BigMoney-Jobs into roles. For example, we could choose to include roles like Part-Timer,

Full-Timer and Contractor. In the rest of this chapter we'll look at how to come up with a list of roles and how to refine that list so that it is useful.

Role Modeling Steps

We will use the following steps to identify and select a useful set of user roles:

- brainstorm an initial set of user roles

- organize the initial set

- consolidate roles

- refine the roles

Each of these steps is discussed in the following sections.

Brainstorming an Initial Set of User Roles

To identify user roles, the customer and as many of the developers as possible meet in a room with either a large table or a wall to which they can tape or pin cards. It's always ideal to include the full team for the user role modeling that initiates a project but it's not necessary. As long as a reasonable representation of the developers is present along with the customer, you can have a successful session.

Each participant grabs a stack of note cards from a pile placed in the middle of the table. (Even if you plan to store the user roles electronically you should start by writing them on cards.) Start with everyone writing role names on cards and then placing them on a table, or taping or pinning them to a wall.

When a new role card is placed, the author says the name of the new role and nothing more. Since this is a brainstorming session, there is no dicsussion of the cards or evaluation of the roles. Rather, each person writes as many cards as he or she can think of. There are no turns, you don't go around the table asking for new roles. Each participant just writes a card whenever she thinks of a new role.

While brainstorming roles, the room will be filled with sounds of pens scratching on cards and will be punctuated by someone occasionally placing a new card and reading the name of the role. Continue until progress stalls and participants are having a hard time thinking up new roles. At that point you may not have identified all of the roles but you're close enough. Rarely does this need to last longer than fifteen minutes.

A User Role Is One User

When brainstorming a project's roles, stick to identifying roles that represent a single user. For example, for the BigMoneyJobs project it may be tempting to write stories such as "A company can post a job opening." However, since a company as a whole cannot use the software, the story will be better if it refers to a role that represents an individual.

Organizing the Initial Set

Once the group has finished identify roles, it's time to organize them. To do this, cards are moved around on the table or wall so that their positions indicate the relationships between the roles. Overlapping roles are placed so that their cards overlap. If the roles overlap a little, overlap the cards a little. If the roles overlap entirely, overlap the cards entirely. An example is shown in Figure 3.1.

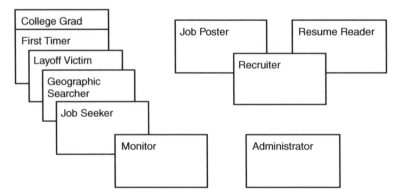

Figure 3.1 *Organizing the user role cards on a table.*

Figure 3.1 shows that the College Grad and First Timer, as those roles were intended by their card writers, overlap signficantly. There's less but similar overlap among the other cards representing people who will use the site to search for jobs. The Monitor role card is shown with only a slight overlap because that role refers to someone who is relatively happy in her current job but likes to keep her eyes open.

To the right of the job-seeking roles in Figure 3.1 are the Job Poster, Recruiter, and Resume Reader role cards. The Recruiter role is shown overlapping both Job Poster and Resume Reader because a recruiter will both post ads and read resumes. An Administrator role is shown also. This role represents users internal to BigMoneyJobs who will support the system.

System Roles

As much as you can, stick with user roles that define people, as opposed to other systems. If you think it will help, then identify an occasional non-human user role. However, the purpose of identifying user roles is to make sure that we think really hard about the users that we absolutely, positively must satisfy with the new system. We don't need user roles for every conceivable user of the system, but we need roles for the ones who can make or break the success of the project. Since other systems are rarely purchasers of our system, they can rarely make or break the success of our system. Naturally, there can be exceptions to this and if you feel that adding a non-human user role helps you think about your system, then add it.

Consolidating Roles

After the roles have been grouped, try to consolidate and condense the roles. Start with cards that are entirely overlapping. The authors of overlapping cards describe what they meant by those role names. After a brief discusson the group decides if the roles are equivalent. If equivalent, the roles can either be consolidated into a single role (perhaps taking its name from the two initial roles), or one of the initial role cards can be ripped up.

In Figure 3.1 the College Grad and First Timer roles are shown as heavily overlapping. The group decides to rip up the College Grad card since any stories for that user role would likely be identical to stories for a First Timer. Even though First Timer, Layoff Victim, Geographic Searcher and Job Seeker have significant overlap, the group decides that each represents a constituency that will be important to satisfy and the roles will have important but subtly different goals for how they use the BigMoneyJobs website.

When they look at the right side of Figure 3.1, the group decides that it is not worth distinguishing between a Job Poster and a Resume Reader. They decide that a Recruiter covers these two roles adequately and those cards are ripped up. However, the group decides that there are differences between an Internal Recruiter (working for a specific company) and an External Recruiter (matching candidates to jobs at any company). They create new cards for Internal Recruiter and External Recruiter, and consider these as specialized versions of the Recruiter role.

In addition to consolidating overlapping roles, the group should also rip up any role cards for roles that are unimportant to the success of the system. For example, the Monitor role card represents someone who is just keeping an eye on the job market. A Monitor may not switch jobs for three years. BigMoney-Jobs can probably do quite well without paying attention to that user role. They decide they will be better off focusing on the roles that will be important to the success of the company, such as Job Seeker and the Recruiter roles.

After the team has consolidated the cards, they are arranged on the table or wall to show relationships between the roles. Figure 3.2 shows one of many possible layouts for the BigMoneyJobs role cards. Here a generic role, such as Job Seeker or Recruiter, is positioned above specialized versions of that role. Alternatively, cards can be stacked or positioned in any other way that the group desires in order to show whatever relationships they think are important.

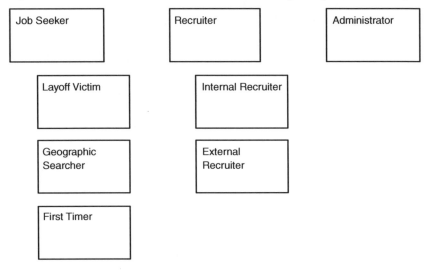

Figure 3.2 *The consolidated role cards.*

Refining the Roles

Once we've consolidated roles and have a basic understanding for how the roles relate to each other, it is possible to model those roles by defining attributes of each role. A role attribute is a fact or bit of useful information about the users who fulfill the role. Any information about the user roles that distinguishes one role from another may be used as a role attribute. Here are some attributes worth considering when preparing any role model:

- The frequency with which the user will use the software.

- The user's level of expertise with the domain.

- The user's general level of proficiency with computers and software.

- The user's level of proficiency with the software being developed.

- The user's general goal for using the software. Some users are after convenience, others favor a rich experience, and so on.

Beyond these standard attributes you should consider the software being built and see if there are any attributes that might be useful in describing its users. For instance, for the BigMoneyJobs website you may want to consider whether the user role will be looking for a part-time or full-time job.

As you identify interesting attributes for a role, write notes on the role card. When finished, you can hang the role cards in a common area used by the team so they can be used as reminders. A sample user role card is shown in Figure 3.3.

User Role: Internal Recruiter

Not particularly computer-savvy but quite adept at using the Web. Will use the software infrequently but intensely. Will read ads from other companies to figure out how to best word her ads. Ease of use is important, but more importantly what she learns must be easily recalled months later.

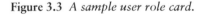

Figure 3.3 *A sample user role card.*

Two Additional Techniques

We could stop right now if we want to. By now a team might have spent an hour—almost certainly no more than that—and they will have put more thought into the users of their software than probably 99% of all software teams. Most teams should, in fact, stop at this point. However, there are two additional techniques that are worth pointing out because they may be helpful in thinking about users on some projects. Only use these techniques if you can anticipate a direct, tangible benefit to the project.

Personas

Identifying user roles is a great leap forward, but for some of the more important user roles, it might be worth going one step further and creating a *persona* for the role. A persona is an imaginary representation of a user role. Earlier in this chapter we met Mario who is responsible for posting new job openings for his company. Creating a persona requires more than just adding a name to a user role. A persona should be described sufficiently that everyone on the team feels like they know the persona. For example, Mario may be described as follows:

> Mario works as a recruiter in the Personnel department of Speedy-Networks, a manufacturer of high-end networking components. He's worked for SpeedyNetworks six years. Mario has a flex-time arrangement and works from home every Friday. Mario is very strong with computers and considers himself a power user of just about all the products he uses. Mario's wife, Kim, is finishing her Ph.D. in chemistry at Stanford University. Because SpeedyNetworks has been growing almost consistently, Mario is always looking for good engineers.

If you choose to create personas for your project, be careful that enough market and demographic research has been done that the personas chosen truly represent the product's target audience.

This persona description gives us a good introduction to Mario. However, nothing speaks as loudly as a picture, so you should also find a picture of Mario and include that with the persona definition. You can get photographs all over the web or you can cut one from a magazine. A solid persona definition combined with a photograph will give everyone on the team a thorough introduction to the persona.

Most persona definitions are too long to fit on a note card, so I suggest you write them on a piece of paper and hang them in the team's common space. You do not need to write persona definitions for every user role. You may, however, think about writing a persona definition for one or two of the primary user roles. If the system you are building is such that it is absolutely vital that the product satisfy one or two user roles, then those user roles are candidates for expansion into personas.

Stories become much more expressive when put in terms of a user role or persona. After you have identified user roles and possibly a persona or two, you can begin to speak in terms of roles and personas instead of the more generic "the user." Rather than writing stories like "A user can restrict job searches to specific geographic regions" you can write "A Geographic Searcher can restrict his job searches to a specific geographic region." Hopefully writing a story this way reminds the team about Allan who is looking for any job on Maui. Writing some stories with user role or persona names does not mean that other roles cannot perform those stories; rather, it means that there is some benefit in thinking about a specific user role or persona when discussing or coding the story.

Extreme Characters

Djajadiningrat and co-authors (2000) have proposed a second technique you might want to think about: the use of extreme characters when considering the design of a new system. They describe an example of designing a Personal Digital Assistant (PDA) handheld computer. They advise that instead of designing solely for a typical sharp-dressed, BMW-driving management consultant, the system designers should consider users with exaggerated personalities. Speficially, the authors suggest designing the PDA for a drug dealer, the Pope, and a twenty-year-old woman who is juggling multiple boyfriends.

It is very possible that considering extreme characters will lead you to stories you would be likely to miss otherwise. For example, it is easy to imagine that the drug dealer and a woman with several boyfriends may each want to maintain multiple separate schedules in case the PDA is seen by the police or a boyfriend. The Pope probably has less need for secrecy but may want a larger font size.

So, while extreme characters may lead to new stories, it is hard to know whether those stories will be ones that should be included in the product. It is probably not worth much investment in time, but you might want to experiment with extreme characters. At a minimum, you can have a few minutes of fun thinking about how the Pope might use your software and it just may lead to an insight or two.

What If I Have On-Site Users?

The user role modeling techniques described in this chapter are still useful even if you have real, live users in your building. Working with real users will strongly improve your likelihood of delivering the desired software. However, even with real users there is no guarantee that you have the right users or the right mix of users.

To decrease the likelihood of failing to satisfy important users, you should do some simple role modeling on projects even when you have available internal users.

Summary

- Most project teams consider only a single type of user. This leads to software that ignores the needs of at least some user types.

- To avoid writing all stories from the perspective of a single user, identify the different user roles who will interact with the software.

- By defining relevant attributes for each user role, you can better see the differences between roles.

- Some user roles benefit from being described by personas. A persona is an imaginary representation of a user role. The persona is given a name, a face, and enough relevant details to make them seem real to the project members.

- For some applications, extreme characters may be helpful in looking for stories that would otherwise be missed.

Developer Responsibilities

- You are responsible for participating in the process of identifying user roles and personas.

- You are responsible for understanding each of the user roles or personas and how they differ.

- While developing the software, you are responsible for thinking about how different user roles may prefer the software to behave.

- You are responsible for making sure that identifying and describing user roles does not go beyond its role as a tool in the process.

Customer Responsibilities

- You are responsible for looking broadly across the space of possible users and identifying appropriate user roles.

- You are responsible for participating in the process of identifying user roles and personas.

- You are responsible for ensuring that the software does not focus inappropriately on a subset of users.

- When writing stories you will be responsible for ensuring that each story can be associated with at least one user role or persona.

- While developing the software, you are responsible for thinking about how different user roles may prefer the software to behave.

- You are responsible for making sure that identifying and describing user roles does not go beyond its role as a tool in the process.

Questions

3.1   Take a look at the eBay website. What user roles can you identify?

3.2   Consolidate the roles you came up with in the previous question and show how you would lay out the role cards. Explain your answer.

3.3   Write persona descriptions for the one most important user role.

Chapter 4

Gathering Stories

How do you gather the stories? This chapter offers advice on working with users in order to identify stories in your conversations with them. The advantages of various approaches will be described. This chapter describes effective methods for getting at a user's real needs by asking the right types of questions.

Elicitation and Capture Should Be Illicit

Even some of the best books on requirements use words like *elicitation* (Kovitz 1999; Lauesen 2002; Wiegers 1999) and *capture* (Jacobson, Booch and Rumbaugh 1999) to describe the practice of identifying requirements. Terms like these imply requirements are out there somewhere and all we need to do is have them explained to us and then we can lock them in a cage. Requirements are not out there in the project space waiting to be captured. Similarly, it is not the case that users already know all the requirements and we need only elicit them.

Robertson and Robertson (1999) introduce the term trawling to describe the process of gathering requirements. Trawling for requirements leads to the mental image that requirements are captured in a fishing net being pulled behind a boat. This metaphor works on a variety of levels.

First, it is consistent with the idea that different-sized nets can be used to capture different-sized requirements. A first pass can be made over the requirements pond with a large mesh net to get all the big ones. You can get a feel for the needed software from the big requirements and then make a subsequent pass with a smaller mesh net and get the medium-sized requirements, still leaving the small ones for later. This metaphor works whether we think of size as business value, essentialness to the software, and so on.

Second, trawling for requirements expresses the idea that requirements, like fish, mature and possibly die. My net may miss a requirement today because the requirement is not important to the system. However, as the system grows in unpredictable directions based on the feedback from each iteration, some requirements will grow in importance. Similarly, other requirements that were once considered important will decrease in importance to the point where we can consider them dead.

Third, just like you won't catch all of the fish in an area by trawling, you won't capture all of the requirements. However, just as with trawling for fish, when you trawl for requirements you are likely to capture the flotsam and jet-sam that bloat requirements.

Finally, the metaphor of trawling for requirements captures the important reality that skill plays a factor in finding the requirements. A skilled require-ments trawler will know where to look for requirements, while the unskilled trawler will waste time with inefficient techniques or in the wrong locations. This chapter is about learning the techniques that make us efficient in trawling for user stories.

A Little Is Enough, or Is It?

One of the easiest ways to spot a traditional prescriptive process is to look at its approach to requirements. Prescriptive processes are characterized by their heavy emphasis on getting all the requirements right and written early in the project. Agile projects, on the other hand, acknowledge that it is impossible to use a net with such a fine mesh that we can get all of the user stories in one pass. Agile processes also acknowledge that there is a time dimension to stories: the relevance of a story changes based on the passage of time and on what sto-ries were added to the product in prior iterations.

However, even though we acknowledge the impossibility of writing all of the stories for a project, we should still make an initial upfront attempt to write those that we can, even if many are written at a very high level. One of the advantages of working with stories is that it is very easy to write them at differ-ent levels of detail. We can write "A user can search for jobs" either as a place-holder or because that's all we know at the time. We can then evolve that story into smaller, more useful stories later. Because of this, it is very easy to write sto-ries for a large portion of an application with less work than with other require-ments techniques.

This is not a recommendation to start a new project by spending three months writing user stories. Rather, it means to look into the future for approx-imately one release (perhaps three to six months) and then write user stories that decrease in detail as the time horizon increases. For example, if the customer or users have said they "probably want reports in this release" then write a card that simply says "A user can run reports." But stop there: don't determine if they need to configure their own reports, whether reports are formatted in HTML, or whether reports can be saved.

Similarly, it is often important to get an overall feel for the size of an application long in advance of starting it. It is often necessary to have a rough idea of what a project will cost and what benefits it will deliver before getting funding and approval to start the project. To know the answers to these questions requires at least a little forethought into the stories that will comprise the project.

Techniques

Because stories will be evolving, coming and going throughout the project, we need a set of techniques for gathering them that can be used iteratively. The techniques we use must be sufficiently lightweight and non-obtrusive that they can be applied more or less continuously. Some of the most valuable techniques for creating a set of stories are:

- User interviews

- Questionnaires

- Observation

- Story-Writing workshops

Many of these techniques are in the toolkit of the traditional business analyst. Projects with a business analyst available should make use of her to do much of the trawling for stories.

Each of these techniques will be considered in the following sections.

User Interviews

Interviewing users is the default approach many teams take to trawling for stories and is probably one you will want to use. One of the keys to success with interviews is the selection of interviewees. As discussed in Chapter 5, "Working with User Proxies," there are many user proxies available; but you should obviously interview real users whenever possible. You should also interview users who fill different user roles.

It is not sufficient to ask the user "So, what do you need?" Most users are not very adept at understanding, and especially at expressing, their true needs. I learned this once from a user who walked into my office and acknowledged, "You built exactly what I asked for but it's not what I want."

I worked with a team that was developing software for delivering surveys. Each survey would be delivered over the phone, via email, and via interactive voice response. Different types of users would use different survey types. The surveys were very complicated: specific answers to one set of questions would determine which question would be asked next. The users needed a way to enter the surveys and they presented the development team with examples of a complicated mini-language they proposed using to formulate questions. This entirely text-based approach seemed needlessly complicated to one of the developers. The developer showed the users how they could instead create surveys visually by dragging and dropping icons that represented different types of questions in a survey. The users ripped up their mini-language and worked with the developers to create a visual survey design tool. Just because these users had the problem does not mean they were uniquely qualified to propose its solution.

Open-Ended and Context-Free Questions

The best technique for getting to the essence of a user's needs is through the questions you ask. I worked with a project team that was torn between putting their application in a browser or writing it as a more traditional platform-specific program. They struggled between the ease-of-deployment and lower training costs provided by the browser-based version and the more powerful platform-specific client. The intended users would certainly like the advantages of the browser, but they also valued the richer user experience provided by the platform-specific client.

It was suggested that the target users for the product be asked their preference. Since the product would be a new generation rewrite of a legacy product, the marketing group agreed to contact a representative sample of current users. Each user in the survey was asked "Would you like our new application in a browser?"

This question was like going to your favorite restaurant and having the waiter ask if you'd like to have your meal for free. Of course, you would! And of course the surveyed users responded that they would love to have the new version of the software in a browser.

The mistake the marketing group made was that they asked a closed-ended question and failed to provide sufficient detail for it to be answered. The question assumed that anyone being interviewed would know the tradeoffs between the browser and the unstated alternatives. A better version of the question would have been:

> Would you like our new application in a browser rather than as a native Windows application even if it means reduced performance, a poorer overall user experience, and less interactivity?

This question still has a problem because it is closed-ended. The respondent is given no room for anything other than a simple yes or no. It is far better to ask open-ended questions that let respondents express more in-depth opinions. For example, "What would you be willing to give up in order to have our next generation product run within a browser?" A user answering that question can go in a variety of directions. Where she goes—and does not go—with her answer will provide you with a more meaningful answer to the question.

It is equally important to ask context-free questions, which are ones that do not include an implied answer or preference. For example, you would not ask, "You wouldn't be willing to trade performance and a rich user experience just for having the software in a browser, would you?" It's pretty clear how most people are going to answer that question.

Similarly, instead of asking "How fast do searches need to be?" ask "What kind of performace is required?" or "Is performance more important in some parts of the application?" The first question is not context-free because it implies there is a performance requirement to searching. There may not have been but, having been asked, a user is unlikely to say so; she's more likely to take a guess.

At some point you will need to move from context-free questions to very specific questions. However, by starting with context-free questions you leave open the possibility for a wider range of answers from users. That will lead you to stories that may have remained undiscovered if you jumped right into very specific questions.

Questionnaires

Questionnaires can be an effective technique for gathering information about stories you already have. If you have a large user population, then a questionnaire can be a great way to get information about how to prioritize the stories. Questionnaires are similarly useful when you need answers from a large number of users to specific questions.

However, questionnaires are usually inappropriate as a primary technique of trawling for new stories. Questionnaires do not lend themselves to followup questions. Also, unlike in a conversation, it is impossible to follow a user down an interesting path that comes up.

As an example use of a questionnaire, you may survey current users about how often they use features in the software today and what their reasons are for not using some feature more. This may lead to prioritizing some usability stories higher than they have been prioritized in the past. As another example, a questionnaire that asked "What new features would you like to see?" will be of limited use. If you give the user a list of choices then you may miss hearing about the five critical features you've never thought of. Alternatively, if the user is allowed to respond with free-form text it will be difficult to tabulate answers.

Given their one-way communication nature and inherent time lag, I do not recommend using questionnaires when trawling for stories. If you want to gather information from a broad base of existing users and can wait one or more iterations to incorporate the information, then use them in that manner but not as a primary means of gathering stories.

Observation

Observing users interact with your software is a wonderful way to pick up insights. Every time I have had the chance to observe someone using my software, I have left flush with ideas about how to improve their experience, productivity, or both. Unfortunately, opportunities for user observation are rare unless you are developing for in-house customers. Too many commercial products take the approach that it's possible to guess what users want. If you have the chance to observe users work with your software, take it. This chance for rapid and direct feedback from users is one of many reasons to release software as early and often as possible.

At one company the users were nurses working in a call center. The nurses answered medical questions from callers. The nurses indicated that they needed a large text field that could be used for documenting the results of the call when the call was finished. An initial version of the software included a large text field on the call wrapup screen. However, after the initial release each member of the development team spent a day observing the users. One of the things discovered was that the large text field was used for entry of things that could have been tracked by the system. By observing the users, the developers discovered that the real need was for the system to track the decisions made by the user as she worked with the software. The large text field was replaced with a feature that logged all searches and recommendations the nurse selected. The real need—tracking all instructions given to a caller—had been obscured by the nurses' description of the need and only came out during observation.

Story-Writing Workshops

A story-writing workshop is a meeting that includes developers, users, the product customer and other parties who can contribute by writing stories. During the workshop the participants write as many stories as they can. No priorities are associated with the stories at this point; the customer will have a chance to do that later. In my opinion, a story-writing workshop is the most effective way to quickly trawl for stories. At a minimum, I recommend conducting a story-writing workshop prior to starting each planned release. You can always hold additional workshops while working toward the release but that typically is not necessary.

A properly conducted story-writing workshop can be a very rapid way to write a great number of stories. From my experience, a good story-writing workshop combines the best elements of brainstorming with low-fidelity prototyping. A low-fidelity prototype is done on paper, note cards, or a white board and maps very high level interactions within the planned software. The prototype is built up iteratively during the workshop as the participants brainstorm the things a user may want to do at various points while using the application. The idea is not to identify actual screens and fields, as in traditional prototyping or Joint Application Design (JAD) sessions. Rather, the conceptual workflows are identified. Figure 4.1 shows the start of a low-fidelity prototype for the BigMoneyJobs website.

Each box represents a new component of the website. The component's title is underlined in the box. Below the title is a very short list of what the component does or contains. The arrows between the boxes represent links between the components. For a website, a component may be either a new page or space on the current page. So, a link indicates that a new page appears or that the information is displayed on the same web page. For example, Search Jobs may be a page on its own or it may be an area on the home page. The distinction is not important, as the customer and developers will have plenty of time to discuss specifics like that later.

To start a low fidelity prototype, first decide which of the system's user roles or personas you'd like to start with. You'll repeat the process using each role or persona so the order does not matter. Next, draw an empty box and tell the participants that it is the main screen of the software, and ask them what the selected user role or persona can do from there. It does not matter that you haven't figured out what the main screen is yet and what's active on that screen. The meeting participants will start throwing out ideas about what actions the role or persona can take. For each action, draw a line to a new box, label that box, and write a story.

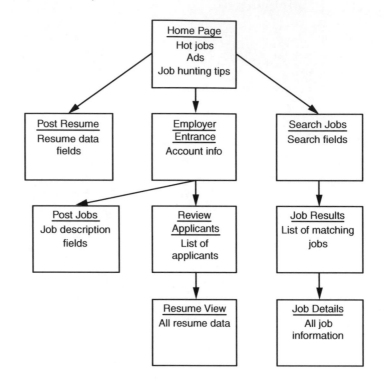

Figure 4.1 *A low-fidelity prototype for BigMoneyJobs.*

The discussion that led to the creation of Figure 4.1 will generate stories such as:

- A Job Seeker can post her resume.

- An Employer can post jobs.

- An Employer can review submitted resumes.

- A Job Seeker can search for jobs.

- A Job Seeker can view results of jobs that match a search.

- A Job Seeker can view details about specific jobs.

None of these stories requires knowledge about how the screens will be designed. However, walking through the workflows will help everyone involved think of as many stories as possible. I have found it most efficient to take a depth-first approach: For the first component, write down its salient details, then move to a component connected to the first and do the same. Then, move to a component connected to that one, rather than going back to the first component and first describing each component connected to it. Using a breadth-first approach can be somewhat disorienting as it becomes hard to remember where you left off in pursuing each path to its end.

Thow It Away

Be sure to throw away or erase the low-fidelity prototype within a few days of creating it. A prototype is not a long-term artifact of your development process and you don't want to cause any confusion by keeping it around. If you leave a story-writing workshop with the feeling that you didn't finish, then keep the prototype around for a few more days, revisit it, try to write any missing stories, and then get rid of it.

A low-fidelity prototype does not need to go into the trash at the end of the day that you created it. But it needs to end up there soon.

As you walk through the prototype, ask questions that will help you identify missing stories, such as:

- What will the user most likely want to do next?

- What mistakes could the user make here?

- What could confuse the user at this point?

- What additional information could the user need?

Think about the user roles and personas as you ask these questions. Many of the answers can change based on the user role being considered.

Maintain a parking lot of issues to come back to. For example, in discussing BigMoneyJobs someone may ask if the system will support contract workers as well as full-time employees. If no one has thought of that prior to the workshop, write it down some place where you can see it and can come back to it later—either at the end of the workshop or after some followup work after the workshop.

During a story writing workshop the focus should be on quantity rather than quality. Even if you'll eventually keep your stories electronically, during the story-writing workshop use cards. Just let the ideas come and write them down. A story that seems like a bad idea now might seem brilliant in a few hours or it may be the inspiration for another story. Additionally, you do not want to get bogged down in lengthy debate over each story. If a story is redundant with or becomes replaced by a better story later, then you can just rip up the story. Similarly, when the customer prioritizes stories for a release, she can assign a low priority to low quality stories.

Occasionally some participants in a story-writing workshop have a hard time either getting started or moving past a sticking point. In this case it can be very beneficial to have access to competitive or similar products.

Pay attention to who is contributing during a story writing workshop. Occasionally a participant will remain silent through much or all of the meeting. If this is the case, talk to the participant during one of the breaks and make sure she's comfortable with the process. Some participants are reluctant to speak up in front of their peers or supervisors, which is why it is important that story ideas not be judged during these sessions. Once participants become comfortable that their ideas will simply be noted, not debated, at this point they will contribute more readily.

Finally, let me reiterate that discussion during a user story workshop should remain at a very high level. The goal is to write as many user stories in as short a time as possible. This is not the time to design screens or solve problems.

Summary

- The idea of eliciting and capturing requirements is wrong. It leads to the twin fallacies that users already know all the requirements and that requirements can be captured and locked in a cage where they will remain unchanged.

- The metaphor of trawling for requirements is far more useful: it captures the ideas that there are different sizes of requirements, that requirements may change over time, and that it takes skill to find the requirements.

- While agile processes are supportive of requirements that emerge late in the process, you should still start by looking forward to approximately the end of the intended release and write the user stories you can easily see.

- User stories can be found by interviewing users, observing users, questionnaires, and holding story-writing workshops.

- The best results are acheived by using a combination of methods rather than overreliance on any one method.

- The most useful answers are given in response to open-ended, context-free questions, such as "Tell me about how you'd like to search for a job" rather than "Will you search for a job by title?"

Developer Responsibilities

- You are responsible for understanding and using multiple techniques while trawling for user stories.

- You are responsible for knowing how to best make use of open-ended and context-free questions.

Customer Responsibilities

- You are responsible for understanding and using multiple techniques while trawling for user stories.

- You are responsible for writing as many user stories as early as possible.

- As the main representative of the software's users, you are responsible for understanding your options in communicating with them.

- You are responsible for knowing how to best make use of open-ended and context-free questions.

- If you need or want help in writing the stories, you are responsible for scheduling and running one or more story-writing workshops.

- You are responsible for making sure all user roles are appropriately represented while trawling for stories.

Questions

4.1   What problems would you expect if a team only gathered requirements through the use of questionnaires?

4.2   Rephrase the following questions to be context free and open-ended. Do you think the user should have to enter a password? Should the system automatically save the user's work every 15 minutes? Can one user see database entries saved by another user?

4.3   Why is it best to ask open-ended, context-free questions?

Chapter 5

Working with User Proxies

It is vital that a project include one or more real users on the customer team. While others may be able to guess at how a user wants the software to behave, only a real user knows. Unfortunately, it is often difficult to get the users we need. For example, we might be developing a shrinkwrap product with users across the country but be unable to bring one (or more) of them onsite with us to write the stories. Or we might be writing software that will be used within our company, but someone tells us we cannot talk to the users. When we cannot get as many users as we want to represent different perspectives of the product, we need to resort to *user proxies*, who may not be users themselves but are on a project to help represent users.

Selection of appropriate user proxies can be critical to the success of the project. The background and motives of possible user proxies must be considered. A user proxy with a marketing background will approach the stories differently than will a user proxy who is a domain expert. It is important to be aware of these differences. In this chapter we will consider various user proxy types who may sometimes fill in for real users.

The Users' Manager

When doing development on a project for internal use, the organization may be reluctant to give you full and unlimited access to one or more users but may be willing to give you access to the users' manager. Consider this a bait-and-switch unless the manager is also a true user of the software. Even then, it is almost certain that the manager has different usage patterns of the software than does a typical user. For example, on one call center application the team was initially given access to shift supervisors. While shift supervisors did use the software, many of the features they wanted in a new version were focused around managing call queues and transferring calls between agents. These features were of

55

very minimal importance to the users they supervised, for whom the software was mostly intended. If the developers had not pushed for direct access to more typical users, the supervisors' less frequently used features would have been overemphasized in the product.

Sometimes the users' manager intercedes and wants to play the user role on the project because of her ego. She may acknowledge that she's not a typical user but will insist that she knows more about what her users need than they do. Naturally, though, in this type of situation you will need to be careful not to offend the user's manager. But you do need to find a way at least partially around her and to the end users for the project to succeed. Some ideas for this are given later in this chapter in the section "What to Do When Working with a User Proxy" on page 61.

Five Minutes Does Not Equal One Minute

The "user" on this internal project was a Vice President who never used the software and had a level of managers between her and the end users. In prioritizing stories for the next iteration, she wanted the developers to focus on improving the speed of the database queries. The team noted the story and its high priority but they were puzzled. They knew application performance was critical and had built a monitoring mechanism into the software: each time a database query was executed, its parameters, the time it took to execute, and the name of the user were stored in the database. This information was monitored at least once a day and there had been no indications of a performance problem. Yet their "user" had told them that some queries were taking "up to five minutes."

After the meeting with the Vice President, the team looked into the query execution history. Here's what they found: A couple of users had in fact executed queries that took one minute to complete. That was certainly longer than desired but considering what they were searching for, the size of the database, and the infrequency of that type of search, it was within the expected performance of the system. But the users had reported the one-minute query to their manager. The manager then reported it to the Vice President; but to make sure the problem got the Vice President's attention, the manager said queries were taking two minutes. Then the Vice President reported it to the developers, and to make sure she got their attention, increased the problem to "up to five minutes."

Users' managers can be sources of misinformation. Whenever possible, corroborate their statements by talking to real users.

A Development Manager

A development manager is one of the worst possible choices to act as a proxy user, unless perhaps you are writing software targeted at development managers. While the development manager may have nothing but the most honorable intentions, it is far too likely that she will also have some conflicting goals. For example, the development manager may prioritize stories differently than would a real user because doing so allows her to accelerate the introduction of an exciting, new technology. Additionally, the development manager may have unaligned corporate goals: perhaps her annual bonus is tied to a completion date on the project, which could cause her to consider the project complete before a real user would.

Finally, most development managers simply do not have hands-on experience as users of the software they are building and are not domain experts. If your prospective user is a development manager who does have domain expertise, then consider her a domain expert and read the discussion in the "Domain Experts" section of this chapter before deciding if you have an adequate user proxy.

Salespersons

The danger in using a salesperson as a user proxy is that it does not lead to a comprehensive view of the product to be built. The most important story to a salesperson will usually be the story whose absence cost her the last sale. If she lost a sale because the product does not have an undo feature, you can bet that the undo story card will be instantly sorted right to the top of the pile. Depending on the importance of a specific lost sale, it may be desirable to write a new story or two; however, a product development company that puts too much emphasis on each lost sale may lose track of whatever strategic, long-term vision is held for the product.

Salespeople are, however, a great conduit to users and you should use them in this way. Ask them to introduce you to customers either on the phone or while along on a sales visit. Even better, attend an industry trade show and work in your company's exhibit.

Talk to Your Users

In 1995 this team was challenged with creating what would be one of the web's first general health information sites. Because there were not yet any competitors, the team could not look to them for story ideas. The user proxy for the project was a director with a marketing background. Because of his marketing background, he understood the importance of talking with prospective users to find out what they would want in a health information site. However, because of the pressure to deliver the site quickly, he plunged forward and built the site using only his gut feel to guide him.

As you can guess, the project didn't fulfill its users' needs. About a month after the site launched I walked into the marketing director's office. He pointed to his monitor and said, "Look at that. Just look at that." On his screen was a porn site. After a moment I asked why we were looking at it. I don't think he'd even noticed the porn on the site. His eyes were fixed on a hit counter and he said, "Just look, they've had 100,000 hits since yesterday. We've had 200."

If you want your software to be used, you have to talk to those who will use it.

Domain Experts

Domain experts, sometimes called subject matter experts, are critical resources because of how well they understand the domain the software will be targeted at. Naturally some domains are harder to understand than others. I used to write a lot of software for attorneys and paralegals, and while the software was sometimes complex, I could usually understand what they were asking for. Much later, I was involved with writing software for statistical geneticists. This domain was filled with words like phenotype, centimorgan, and haplotype. These were words I had never heard before, which made the domain much harder to grasp. This made each of the developers much more reliant on a domain expert to help us understand what we were developing.

While domain experts are great resources, their usefulness is really dependent upon whether they are current or former users of the software type you are building. For example, when building a payroll system you will undoubtedly want to have a Certified Public Accountant (CPA) available as a domain expert. However, since the users will probably be payroll clerks and not CPAs, you will probably get better stories from the payroll clerks. Domain experts are ideal resources when building a domain model and identifying business rules, but workflow and usage issues are better derived from actual users.

Another potential problem with using a domain expert as your user proxy is that you may end up with software aimed only at users with similar levels of domain expertise. Domain experts can be inclined to point the project toward a solution that is suitable for them but is too complex or is just plain wrong for the targeted user audience.

The Marketing Group

Larry Constantine and Lucy Lockwood (1999) point out that marketing groups understand markets rather than users. This can lead a marketing group, or someone with a marketing background, to focus more on the quantity of features in the product than on the quality of those features. In many cases a marketing group may provide useful high-level guidance about relative priorities, but often does not have the insight to provide specific details about the stories.

Former Users

A former user can be great as a proxy if her experience is very recent. However, as with other user proxies, you should carefully consider whether the former user's goals and incentives are fully aligned with those of the real users.

Customers

Customers are those who make the buying decision; they are not necessarily users of the software. It is important to consider the desires of your customers because they, not your users, are the ones who write the check to buy the software. (Unless, of course, your users and customers are the same people.)

Corporate desktop productivity software is a perfect example of the distinction between customer and user. The corporate IT staff may decide which word processor is used by all the employees of the company. In this case, the IT staff is the customer but all employees of the company are users (including the IT staff, who are both customer and user). The features in a product like this must be sufficient that the users do not scream too loudly; but the features must also be those that appeal to the customer making the buying decision.

Talk to Your Users Redux

In one company the marketing group was serving as a customer proxy for a new product that would replace the company's current paper-based product. The company had a very successful history selling printed books containing rules that hospitals and insurance companies had agreed upon: if the hospital followed the rules they would be reimbursed by the insurance company. For example, an appendectomy was only called for if (among other things) a patient's white blood count was above a certain threshold.

The marketing group had no interest in talking to the users of the printed books to find out what they might want the software to do. Instead they reasoned that they knew exactly what their users would want and development could proceed under the guidance of the marketing group. The marketing group chose a book metaphor for the software. Rather than take advantage of the inherent flexibility of software, they settled for an "automated book." The users were, quite obviously, disappointed with the software. Unfortunately, the company could have known this very early on if they had used real users rather than a marketing department as a user proxy.

For example, security features are typically unimportant to most users of desktop productivity software. Security is vitally important, however, to the IT staff (the customers) who make the buying decision.

One project team I worked with had designed a database-intensive application. Data would be loaded into the system from other systems the customers already had. The developers needed to specify a file format that would be used to exchange this data. In this case the customer was the CIO of the organization; the users of this functionality were the IT staff in his organization who would write the extract program to move data from their current systems into the format specified for the new system. When asked about his preferences for the file format, the customer (the CIO) decided that XML would be an ideal technology since it was relatively new at the time and was certainly sexier than a non-standard comma-separated value (CSV) file. When the software was delivered, the users (the IT staff) completely disagreed—they would have preferred the much simpler-to-generate CSV file over the XML file. If the development team had got the stories directly from the users, they could have known this and would not have wasted time on the XML format.

Trainers and Technical Support

Trainers and technical support personnel may seem like logical choices to fill in as a user proxy. They spend their days talking to real users so they must certainly know what users want. Unfortunately, if you use a trainer as your user proxy, you will end up with a system that is easy to train. Similarly, if you use someone from technical support, you will end up with a system that is easily supported. For example, someone from technical support may put low priority on the advanced features that she anticipates will lead to increased support work. While training ease and and supportability are good goals, they are most likely not what a true user would prioritize.

Business or Systems Analysts

Many business and systems analysts make good user proxies because they have one foot in the technology world and one foot in the domain of the software. An analyst who can balance these backgrounds and who puts effort into talking with actual users is often an excellent user proxy.

One problem that some analysts exhibit is that they prefer to think about a problem rather than research it. I've worked with too many analysts who believe they can sit in their offices and intuit what users will want without actually talking to those users. Be watchful that the project's analyst talks to users and that she doesn't just make decisions on her own.

A second problem I've occasionally encountered with analysts is a desire to spend too much time in the project's upfront activities. So, where a two-hour role modeling and story writing workshop might be sufficient to fill in details for a release plan extending out four months, some analysts will prefer to instead spend three weeks on these activities.

What to Do When Working with a User Proxy

Although not ideal, it is still possible to write great software with a user proxy rather than a real user. There are a number of techniques you can apply to increase your chances of success in these cases.

When Users Exist But Access Is Limited

If access to real users is blocked and the team is instead told to work through a user proxy who will make all project decisions, the team will need to work with the proxy but also establish a connection to hands-on users. One of the best techniques for doing this is to request permission to start a *user task force*. A user task force consists of any number of real users, from a handful to a couple of dozen. The task force is used as a sounding-board for ideas, but the proxy remains the project's final decision-maker. In most cases the proxy will go along with this, especially as it gives her a safety net to protect her against bad decisions.

Once a user task force is established and staffed with real users, it can typically be used to guide more and more of the day–to–day decisions on the project. You can do this by having a series of meetings to discuss parts of the application and then have the task force identify, write, and prioritize stories.

One project team I worked with was developing a system for internal users and had great success by taking top-level direction from a user proxy, using prototypes to show a user task force, and then acting on feedback generated during user task force meetings. This particular project ran with month-long iterations. The first few days to a week of each iteration was spent prototyping and holding one or more user task force meetings. In this way the user proxy (the users' manager in this case) had fine control over the strategic direction of the project, but the implementation details were moved from her to the user task force.

When There Really Is No User Available

When there really is no user available and you must resort to a user proxy, one valuable technique is to use more than one user proxy. This helps reduce the likelihood of building a system that meets exactly one person's needs. When using more than one user proxy, be sure to use different types of user proxy. For example, combine a domain expert with someone from marketing rather than using two domain experts. You can do this by either having two designated user proxies, or by having one designated user proxy but encouraging her to rely on other, informal user proxies.

If you are developing software that will compete with other commercial products, you can use the competing products as a source for some stories. What features in the competing products get mentioned in reviews? What features are discussed in online newsgroups? Are the features discussed because they are overly complex to use?

I remember arguing a few years ago with a use case advocate about what type of document best expresses the requirements of a system. He argued in favor of a well thought-out use case model. I argued in favor of the user's guide. I have never seen a project that concluded with a perfectly accurate and current use case model even though some have tried. I have seen many projects that conclude with an accurate and current user's guide. If you are writing new software that will compete with existing products, you can learn a great deal by studying the competing products.

Another technique you can use when working with a user proxy rather than real users is to release the product as soon as possible. Even if the release is called preliminary or an early beta, getting it into the hands of users early will help identify inconsistencies between the thinking of your user proxy and your real users. Even better, once the software is in the hands of one or more early adopters, you have now opened up a communication path to those users and can use that to talk with them about upcoming features.

Can You Do It Yourself?

When you cannot find, or get access to, a real user, avoid falling into the trap of thinking you know your users' minds and do not need or can ignore your user proxy. While each type of user proxy has some type of shortcoming that makes her less desirable than a real user, most developers come with even more shortcomings for pretending to be a real user. In general, developers do not have marketing backgrounds that allow them to understand the relative value of features, they do not have the same amount of customer contact as salespeople, they are not domain experts, and so on.

Constituting the Customer Team

First, always remember that a real user beats a proxy any time. Whenever possible place real users on the customer team. However, when you can't get the right mix of real users, supplement the customer team with one or more user proxies. The customer team should be constructed so that the strengths of one member balance the weaknesses of another member. There are four steps in creating a customer team.

First, add real users. If the software is used by different types of users, try to include a user of each type. For example, on one health care application our users were nurses. On our customer team we had users who were regular nurses, oncology specialists, diabetic specialists, and so on.

Second, identify a single project champion or "first among equals" on the customer team. In commercial software companies this is very often a product manager, but it could be someone else. This project champion becomes responsible for coordinating customer team collaboration. All members of the customer team are, to the extent they can achieve, responsible for delivering a consistent message. While there may not be one customer, there must be one customer voice.

Third, determine the factors critical to project success. This will vary from project to project. For example, if the project is to create a next generation version of an existing product, then a critical success factor will be how easily existing users can move to the new system. Supplement the customer team with user proxies with the relevant knowledge, skills, and experience to address the project's critical success factors. In our example of moving existing users to a new system, this might mean adding a trainer to the customer team.

Summary

- In this chapter we learned about different types of user proxies and why no user proxy is as ideal as a true user when it comes to writing *user* stories.

- The users' manager may not be an appropriate user proxy unless she is also a user.

- Development managers make tempting user proxies because they are already involved in the day-to-day detail of the project. However, the development manager is rarely an intended user of the software being built and is therefore a poor choice as a user proxy.

- In product companies, the customer frequently comes from the marketing group. Someone from the marketing group is often a good choice as a user proxy but must overcome the temptation to focus on the quantity rather than quality of features.

- Salespeople can make good customers when they have contact with a broad variety of customers who are also users. Salespeople must avoid the temptation to focus on whatever story could have won the last lost sale. In all cases, salespeople make excellent conduits to users.

- Domain experts can make excellent user proxies but must avoid the temptation to write stories for a product that only someone with their expertise can use.

- Customers, those who make the purchasing decision, can make great user proxies if in close communication with the users for whom they are purchasing the software. Obviously, a customer who is also a user is a fantastic combination.

- In order to be good user proxies, trainers and technical support personnel must avoid the temptation to focus too narrowly on the aspects of the product they see every day.

- This chapter also looked briefly at some techniques for working with user proxies, including the use of user task forces, using multiple user proxies, competitive analysis, and releasing early to get user feedback.

Developer Responsibilities

- You have the responsibility to help your organization select the appropriate customer for the project.

- You are responsible for understanding how different types of user proxies will think about the system being built and how their backgrounds might influence your interactions.

Customer Responsibilities

- If you will not be a user of the software, you are responsible for knowing which categories of user proxy describe you.

- You are responsible for understanding what biases you may bring to the project and for knowing how to overcome them, whether by relying on others or some other means.

Questions

5.1   What problems can result from using the users' manager as a proxy for the users?

5.2   What problems can result from using a domain expert as a proxy for users?

Chapter 6

Acceptance Testing User Stories

One reason for writing acceptance tests is to express many of the details that result from the conversations between customers and developers. Rather than writing lengthy lists of "The system shall…" style requirements statements, tests are used to fill in the details of a user story.

Testing is best viewed as a two-step process: First, notes about future tests are jotted on the back of story cards. This can be done any time someone thinks of a new test. Second, the test notes are turned into full-fledged tests that are used to demonstrate that the story has been been correctly and fully coded.

As an example of test reminders you may write on the back of a card, the story "A company can pay for a job posting with a credit card" may have the following written on the back of its card:

- Test with Visa, MasterCard and American Express (pass).

- Test with Diner's Club (fail).

- Test with good, bad and missing card ID numbers.

- Test with expired cards.

- Test with different purchase amounts (including one over the card's limit).

These test notes capture assumptions made by the customer. Suppose the customer in the BigMoneyJobs example writes the story "A Job Seeker can view details about a specific job." The customer and a developer discuss the story and identify a set of facts that will be displayed about a job—title, description, location, salary range, how to apply, and so on. However, the customer knows that not all companies will provide all of this information and she expects the site to handle missing data. For example, if no salary information is provided, the customer does not even want the "Salary range" label shown on the screen. This should be reflected as a test because the programmer may *assume* that the job posting part of the system will require every job posting to include salary information.

Acceptance tests also provide basic criteria that can be used to determine if a story is fully implemented. Having criteria that tell us when something is done is the best way to avoid putting too much, or too little, time and effort into it. For example, when my wife bakes a cake, her acceptance test is to stick a toothpick into it; if the toothpick comes out clean, the cake is done. I acceptance test her cake by running a finger through the frosting and tasting.

Write Tests Before Coding

Acceptance tests provide a great deal of information that the programmers can use in advance of coding the story. For example, consider "Test with different purchase amounts (including one over the card's limit)." If this test is written before a programmer starts coding, it will remind her to handle cases in which a purchase is declined because of insufficient credit. Without seeing that test, some programmers will forget to support this case.

Naturally, in order for programmers to benefit in this way, the acceptance tests for a story must be written before programming begins on that story. Tests are generally written at the following times:

- whenever the customer and developers talk about the story and want to capture explicit details

- as part of a dedicated effort at the start of an iteration but before programming begins

- whenever new tests are discovered during or after the programming of the story

Ideally, as the customer and developers discuss a story they reflect its details as tests. However, at the start of an iteration the customer should go through the stories and write any additional tests she can think of. A good way to do this is to look at each story and ask questions similar to the following:

- What else do the programmers need to know about this story?

- What am I assuming about how this story will be implemented?

- Are there circumstances when this story may behave differently?

- What can go wrong during the story?

Story Card 6.1 shows an example for a real project that was buidling software for a scanning system. The author of this story has clearly stated what she expects to happen (the newly-scanned pages go into a new document, even if a document is currently open in the software). In this case, the expectation was described as part of the story on the front of the card. It could just as easily have been stated as a test on the back of the card. The important thing is that the expectation is reflected somewhere on the card prior to the programmers starting on the story. If that is not done, it is likely the programmers could have coded different behavior, such as inserting the newly-scanned pages into the current document.

> A user can scan pages and insert them into a new document. If a document is already open, then the app should prompt and close the current document.

■ Story Card 6.1   Conveying expectations to the programmers.

The Customer Specifies the Tests

Because the software is being written to fulfill a vision held by the customer, the acceptance tests need to be specified by the customer. The customer can work with a programmer or tester to actually create the tests, but minimally the customer needs to specify the tests that will be used to know when a story has been correctly developed. Additionally, a development team (especially one with experienced testers on it) will usually augment some of the stories with tests they think of.

Testing Is Part of the Process

I recently worked with a company where the tester got her understanding of the software from the programmers. The programmers would code a new feature, they'd explain it to the tester, and the tester would then validate that the program worked as described. Quite often the program would pass these tests but would then be plagued with errors once users started working with it. The problem, of course, was that the tester was testing that the programmer did what she said she did. Without involvement from customers or users, no one was testing that the software did what they wanted it to do.

With user stories it is vital that testing be viewed as part of the development process, not something that happens "after coding is done." Specifying tests is often a shared responsibility of a product manager and a tester. The product manager will bring her knowledge of the organizational goals driving the project; the tester will bring his suspicious mindset. At the start of an iteration they will get together and specify as many initial tests as they can think of. But it doesn't stop there, and it doesn't stop with them getting together once a week. As the details of a story are worked out, additional tests are specified.

How Many Tests Are Too Many?

The customer should continue to write tests as long as they add value and clarification to the story. It is probably not necessary to write a test to confirm that charges cannot be placed on an expired Visa card if you've already written such a test for expired MasterCards.

Also, keep in mind that a good programming team will have unit tests in place for many of the low-level cases. For example, the programming team should have unit tests that correctly identify February 30 and June 31 as invalid dates. The customer is not responsible for identifying every possible test. The customer should focus her efforts on writing tests that clarify the intent of the story to the developers.

The Framework for Integrated Test

Acceptance tests are meant to demonstrate that an application is acceptable to the customer who has been responsible for guiding the system's development. This means that the customer should be the one to execute the acceptance tests. Minimally, acceptance tests should be executed at the end of each iteration. Because working code from one iteration may be broken by development in a subsequent iteration, it is important to execute acceptance tests from all prior iterations. This means that executing acceptance tests gets more time consuming with each passing iteration. If possible, the development team should look into automating some or all of the acceptance tests.

One excellent tool for automating acceptance tests is Ward Cunningham's Framework for Integrated Test[1], or FIT for short. Using FIT, tests are written in a familiar spreadsheet or tabular format. Bob and Micah Martin have led the development of FitNesse[2], an extension of FIT that makes test writing even easier.

FitNesse (which uses FIT) is rapidly becoming a very popular approach for writing acceptance tests on agile projects. Because tests are expressed in spreadsheet-like tables within web pages, the effort for customers to identify and write tests is greatly reduced. Table 6.1 is a sample of the type of table that can be processed by these tools. Each row represents one set of data. In this case the first data row identifies a Visa card that expires in May of 2005 and has the number 4123456789011. The final column indicates whether this card should pass a validity check in the application.[3] In this case the card is expected to be considered valid by the application.

Table 6.1 *Testing for valid credit cards with a table that can be used by FIT and FitNesse.*

CardType	Expiration	Number	valid()
Visa	05/05	4123456789011	true
Visa	05/23	4123456789012349	false
MasterCard	12/04	5123456789012343	true
MasterCard	12/98	5123456789012345	false
MasterCard	12/05	42	false
American Express	4/05	341234567890127	true

In order to execute the tests in Table 6.1, a programmer on the team needs to write code to respond to simple FIT commands. She writes code that invokes code in the application being tested to determine the validity of the credit card. However, to write the acceptance tests, the customer only needs to create a simple table like this one that shows data values and expected results.

When the tests in Table 6.1 are run, the results are displayed by coloring the test columns (the last column in this example) either green (for a passed test) or red (for a failed test). FitNesse and FIT make it simple for either a customer or developer to run the acceptance tests.

---

1.   The Framework for Integrated Test, FIT, is available at fit.c2.com.
2.   FitNesse is availabe from fitnesse.org.
3.   For information on credit card validity, see www.beachnet.com/~hstiles/card-type.html.

Types of Testing

There are many types of testing, and the customer and development team should work together to ensure that the appropriate types of testing are occurring. For most systems, story testing is largely functional testing, which ensures that the applicaton functions as expected. There are, however, other types of testing to be considered. For example, you may want to consider any or all of the following:

- User interface testing, which ensures that all of the components of the user interface behave as expected

- Usability testing, which is done to ensure an application that can be easily used

- Performance testing, which is done to gauge how well the application will perform under various workloads

- Stress testing, in which the application is subjected to extreme values of users, transactions, or anything else that may put the application under stress

Testing for Bugs, Not Coverage

On an agile, story-driven project, testing is not the antagonistic activity that it becomes for many teams. There is no "I gotcha" mentality when a bug is found. There is no room for passing the blame when a bug makes it all the way to production. The highly-collaborative, we're–all–in–this–together mentality of the team prevents this.

On an agile project, we test to find and eliminate bugs; we don't necessarily pursue goals of 100% code coverage or testing of all boundary conditions. We use our intuition, our knowledge, and our past experience to guide our test effort.

Testing is done by whoever is best equipped to do the testing. A customer needs to specify the acceptance tests but she does that with assistance and information from the developers and dedicated testers. For example, consider the tests in Table 6.1. The only expired card that is tested is a MasterCard. If we were striving for complete coverage we would also need to test other card types. But when the customer speaks with the developers, she learns that (in this example) all cards are processed identically and testing an invalid card of one type is sufficient. Over time, through frequent communication and through seeing which types of tests fail, everyone on the project learns how best to focus the test effort.

Summary

- Acceptance tests are used to express details that result from conversations between a customer and a developer.

- Acceptance tests document assumptions about the story a customer has that may not have been discussed with a developer.

- Acceptance tests provide basic criteria that can be used to determine if a story is fully implemented.

- Acceptance tests should be written by the customer rather than by a developer.

- Acceptance tests are written before the programmer begins coding.

- Stop writing tests when additional tests will not help clarify the details or intent of the story.

- FIT and FitNesse are excellent tools for writing acceptance tests in a familiar table or spreadsheet format.

Developer Responsibilities

- You may be responsible for automating the execution of acceptance tests if your team chooses to do so.

- You are responsible for thinking about additional acceptance tests when you start development of a new story.

- You are responsible for unit testing your code so that acceptance tests do not need to be specified for all the minutiae of a story.

Customer Responsibilities

- You are responsible for writing the acceptance tests.

- You are responsible for executing the acceptance tests.

Questions

6.1   Who specifies the tests? Who helps?

6.2   Why specify tests before the stories are coded?

Chapter 7

Guidelines for Good Stories

At this point, with a good foundation of what stories are, how to trawl for and write them, how to identify key user roles, and the role of acceptance testing, we turn our attention to some additional guidelines for writing good stories.

Start with Goal Stories

On a large project, especially one with many user roles, it is sometimes difficult to even know where to begin in identifying stories. What I've found works best is to consider each user role and identify the goals that user has for interacting with our software. For example, consider the Job Seeker role in the BigMoney-Jobs example. She really has one top priority goal: find a job. But we may consider that goal to comprise the following goals:

- search for jobs she's interested in (based on skill, salary, location, and so on)

- automate the search process so she doesn't have to search manually each time

- make her resume available so that companies may search for her

- easily apply for any jobs she likes

These goals (which really are high-level stories themselves) can then be used to generate additional stories as needed.

Slice the Cake

When faced with a large story, there are normally many ways of breaking it into smaller pieces. The first inclination of many developers is to split the story along technical lines. For example, suppose the team has decided that the story "A Job Seeker can post a resume" is simply too large to fit in the current iteration and must be split. The developers may want to split it along technical boundaries, such as:

- A Job Seeker can fill out a resume form.

- Information on a resume form is written to the database.

In this case, one story would be done in the current iteration while the other story would be deferred until (presumably) the next iteration. The problem with this is that neither story on its own is very useful to users. The first story says that job seekers can fill out a form but that the data is not saved. Not only is this not useful, it would actually waste users' time. The second story says that the data collected on the form will be written to the database. Without a story to present the form to users, the second story is not useful.

A far better approach is to write the replacement stories such that each provides some level of end–to–end functionality. Bill Wake (2003a) refers to this as "slicing the cake." Each story must have a little from each layer. This leads to splitting "A Job Seeker can post a resume" like this:

- A Job Seeker can submit a resume that includes only basic information such as name, address, education history.

- A Job Seeker can submit a resume that includes all information an employer may want to see.

Stories that represent a full slice of cake are to be preferred over those that do not. There are two reasons for this. First, exercising each layer of an application's architecture reduces the risk of finding last minute problems in one of the layers. Second, although not ideal, an application could conceivably be released for use with only partial functionality as long as the functionality that is included in the release slices all the way through the system.

Write Closed Stories

Soren Lauesen (2002) introduces the idea of closure for tasks in his compendium of requirements techniques. His ideas are equally applicable to user stories. A closed story is one that finishes with the achievement of a meaningful goal and that allows the user to feel she has accomplished something.

For example, suppose the BigMoneyJobs website project includes the story "A recruiter can manage the ads she has placed." This is not a closed story: Managing the ads she's placed is not something that is ever completely done. Instead, it is an ongoing activity. This story can be better constructed as a set of closed stories, such as:

- A recruiter can review resumes from applicants to one of her ads.

- A recruiter can change the expiration date of an ad.

- A recruiter can delete an application that is not a good match for a job.

And so on. Each of these closed stories is a part of the original story that was not closed. After completing one of these closed stories, a user is likely to feel a sense of accomplishment.

The desire to write closed stories has to be tempered against competing needs. Remember that stories also need to be small enough to be estimatable and small enough to be conveniently scheduled into a single iteration. But stories must also be large enough that you avoid capturing details about them any earlier than necessary.

Put Constraints on Cards

Newkirk and Martin (2001) recommend a practice I've found useful. They introduce the practice of annotating a story card with "Constraint" for any story that must be obeyed rather than directly implemented. An example can be seen in Story Card 7.1.

> The system must support peak usage of up to 50 concurrent users.
>
> Constraint

■ Story Card 7.1   An example of a constraint story card.

Other examples of constraints are:

- Do not make it hard to internationalize the software if needed later.

- The new system must use our existing order database.

- The software must run on all versions of Windows.

- The system will achieve uptime of 99.999%.

- The software will be easy to use.

Even though constraint cards do not get estimated and scheduled into iterations like normal cards, they are still useful. Minimally, constraint cards can be taped to the wall where they act as reminders. Even better, acceptance tests can be written to ensure the constraint is not violated. For example, it would not be difficult to write a test for Story Card 7.1. Ideally the team would write this test during one of the first iterations when there's little chance of it being violated. The team would then continue running the test as part of each subsequent iteration. Whenever possible (and it usually is), write automated tests to ensure that constraints are being met.

For more on constraints as a way of specifying nonfunctional requirements see Chapter 16, "Additional Topics."

Size the Story to the Horizon

You want to focus your attention on the areas that most need it. Usually, this means paying more attention to things happening in the near future than to things happening further out. With stories, you do this by writing stories at different levels based on the implementation horizon of the stories. This means, for example, that stories for the next few iterations would be written at sizes that can be planned into those iterations, while more distant stories could be much larger and less precise. For example, suppose at the highest level we've determined that the BigMoneyJobs website will include four stories:

- A Job Seeker can post a resume.

- A Job Seeker can search job openings.

- A Recruiter can post a job opening.

- A Recruiter can search resumes.

The customer has decided that the first iterations will focus on allowing users to post resumes. Only after the bulk of the resume posting functionality has been added will attention be turned to searching for jobs, posting job openings, and searching resumes. This means that the project team and customer will start having the conversations about "A Job Seeker can post a resume."

That story will be expanded as details are discovered through those conversations; the other three high-level stories will be left alone. A possible list of stories then becomes:

- A Job Seeker can add a new resume to the site.

- A Job Seeker can edit a resume that is already on the site.

- A Job Seeker can remove her resume from the site.

- A Job Seeker can mark a resume as inactive.

- A Job Seeker can mark a resume as hidden from certain employers.

- A Job Seeker can see how many times her resume has been viewed.

- … and so on about posting resumes…

- A Job Seeker can search job openings.

- A Recruiter can post job openings.

- A Recruiter can search resumes.

In writing your stories, take advantage of the flexibility of stories to be useful at various levels.

Keep the UI Out as Long as Possible

One of the problems that has plagued every approach to software requirements has been mixing requirements with solution specification. That is, in stating a requirement, a solution is also either explicitly stated or implied. Most commonly this happens with aspects of the user interface. You want to keep the user interface out of your stories as long as possible. For example, consider Story Card 7.2, which is a story from a real system. If this story is to be developed early in the life of the project, it includes too many user interface details. Readers of this story are told about the print dialog, printer lists, and at least four ways of searching.

Eventually it will become inevitable for user interface details to slip into stories. This happens as the software becomes more and more complete, and stories shift away from being entirely new functionality to being modifications or extensions of existing functionality.

For example, consider the story "A user can select dates from a date widget on the search screen." This story may represent three days of work regardless of whether it's done at the start or end of the project. However, it is not a story you'd expect to have at the start of the project before the user interface has even been considered.

> Print dialog allows the user to edit the printer list. The user can add or remove printers from the printer list. The user can add printers either by auto-search or manually specifying the printer DNS name or IP address. An advanced search option also allows the user to restrict his search within specified IP addresses and subnet range.

■ Story Card 7.2   A card with too much user interface detail.

Some Things Aren't Stories

While user stories are a very flexible format that works well for describing much of the functionality of many systems, they are not appropriate for everything. If you need to express some requirements in a form other than user stories, then do so. For example, user interface guidelines are often described in documents with lots of screen captures. Similarly, apart from any user stories, you may want to document and agree upon an interface between important systems, especially if one is being developed by an external vendor.

If you find that some aspect of a system could benefit from expression in a different format, then use that format.

Include User Roles in the Stories

If the project team has identified user roles, they should make use of them in writing the stories. So instead of writing "A user can post her resume" they write "A Job Seeker can post her resume." The difference is minor but writing stories in this way keeps the user in the forefront of the developer's mind. Instead of thinking of bland, faceless, interchangeable users, the developer will begin thinking of real, tangible users whom she needs to satisfy with the software.

Connextra, one of the early adopters of Extreme Programming, incorporated roles into their stories by using a short template. Each story was written in the following format:

I as a (role) want (function) so that (business value)

You may want to experiment with this template or with one of your own. A template like this can help distinguish important from frivolous stories.

Write for One User

Stories are generally most readable when written for a single user. For many stories, writing for one or many users will not make a difference. However, for some stories the difference can be significant. For example, consider the story "Job Seekers can remove resumes from the site." This could be interpreted to mean that one Job Seeker can remove her own resume and possibly the resumes of others.

Normally, this type of issue will become clear when you think about a story with a single user in mind. For example, the story above could be written as "A Job Seeker can remove resumes." When written this way, the problem of one Job Seeker removing resumes of others becomes more apparent, though, and the story can be further improved to "A Job Seeker can remove her own resumes."

Write in Active Voice

User stories are easier to read and understand when written in active voice. For example, rather than saying "A resume can be posted by a Job Seeker" say "A Job Seeker can post a resume."

Customer Writes

Ideally the customer writes the stories. On many projects the developers help out, either by doing the actual writing during an initial story writing workshop or by suggesting new stories to the customer. But, responsibility for writing stories resides with the customer and cannot be passed to the developers.

Additionally, because the customer is responsible for prioritizing the stories that will go into each iteration, it is vital that the customer understand each story. The best way to do this is to write them.

Don't Number Story Cards

The first time we use story cards many of us are tempted to number them. The usual reasoning is that this will help keep track of individual cards or add some level of traceability to stories. For example, when we discover that the story on card 13 is too large we rip up card 13 and replace it with cards 13.1, 13.2, and 13.3. However, numbering story cards adds pointless overhead to the process and leads us into abstract discussions about features that need to be tangible. I'd rather talk about "the story to add user groups" than "story 13." I especially don't want to talk about "story 13.1."

If you feel compelled to number story cards, instead try adding a short title to the card and use the title as shorthand for the rest of the story text.

Don't Forget the Purpose

Don't forget that the main purpose of a story card is to act as a reminder to discuss the feature. Keep these reminders brief. Add the detail you need to remember where to resume a conversation, but do not replace the conversation by adding more detail to the story card.

Summary

- To identify stories, start by considering the goals of each user role in using the system.

- When splitting a story, try to come up with stories that cut through all layers of the application.

- Try to write stories that are of a size where the user feels justified in taking a coffee break after completing the story.

- Augment stories with other requirements gathering or documenting techniques as necessary for the project's domain and environment.

- Create constraint cards and either tape them to a shared wall or write tests to ensure the constraints are not violated.

- Write smaller stories for functionality the team will implement soon, and write broad, high-level stories for functonality further into the future.

- Keep the user interface out of the stories for as long as possible.

- When practical, include the user role when writing the story.

- Write stories in active voice. For example, say "A Job Seeker can post a resume" rather than "A resume can be posted by a Job Seeker."

- Write stories for a single user. Instead of "Job Seekers can remove resumes" write "A Job Seeker can remove her own resumes."

- Have the customer, rather than a developer, write the stories.

- Keep user stories short, and don't forget their purpose as reminders to hold conversations.

- Don't number story cards.

Questions

7.1 Assume the story "A Job Seeker can search for open jobs" is too large to fit into one iteration. How would you split it?

7.2 Which of these stories is appropriately sized and can be considered a closed story?

   a A user can save her preferences.

   b A user can change the default credit card used for purchases.

   c A user can log on to the system.

7.3 What simple changes could improve the story "Users can post their resumes"?

7.4 How would you test the constraint "The software will be easy to use"?

PART II

Estimating and Planning

With an understanding of stories under our collective belts, we can turn our attention to estimating and planning projects with user stories. On almost all projects, we need, or are asked, to provide an estimate of how long the project will take. Marketing campaigns need to be readied, users need to be trained, hardware needs to be purchased and so on. Each of these activities depends upon a project's plans.

In Part II, we will see how to estimate the stories and how to create a high-level release plan for delivery of the highest priority stories. Then we'll see how the release plan is refined with additional detail at the start of each iteration with the additional planning necessary to perform the work of that iteration. Finally, we'll look at ways to measure and monitor the progress of the project so that we can constantly adjust the plan to reflect the knowledge we gain from each iteration.

Chapter 8

Estimating User Stories

No project can go very long before someone starts asking "When will you be done?" The best approach for estimating stories would be one that:

- allows us to change our mind whenever we have new information about a story

- works for both epics and smaller stories

- doesn't take a lot of time

- provides useful information about our progress and the work remaining

- is tolerant of imprecision in the estimates

- can be used to plan releases

Story Points

An approach that satisfies each of these goals is to estimate in *story points*. A nice feature of story points is that each team defines them as they see fit. One team may decide to define a story point as an ideal day of work (that is, a day without any interruptions whatsoever—no meetings, no email, no phone calls, and so on). Another team may define a story point as an ideal week of work. Yet another team may define a story point as a measure of the complexity of the story. Because of the wide variety of meanings for story points, Joshua Kerievsky has suggested that story points represent Nebulous Units of Time, or NUTs.[1]

My preference is to treat a story point as an ideal day of work. We rarely have these ideal days, but thinking about stories in ideal time offers two advan-

---

1. Joshua Kerievsky on extremeprogramming@yahoogroups.com, August 5, 2003.

tages. First, it is easier than estimating in elapsed time. Estimating in elapsed time forces us to consider all other possible impacts on our time, such as the all-company meeting on Tuesday, my dentist appointment on Wednesday, a few hours a day for answering email, and so on. Second, estimating story points in ideal time gives our estimates a slightly better foundation than when they are estimated in entirely nebulous units. Since one of the main purposes of estimating is to be able to answer questions about the overall expected effort in a project, we will eventually need to convert estimates into time. Starting with ideal time makes that conversion a little simpler than starting with an entirely nebulous unit.

Estimate as a Team

Story estimates need to be owned collectively by the team. Later, in Chapter 10, "Planning an Iteration," we'll see that a story comprises multiple tasks and that a task estimate is owned by the individual who will perform the task. Story estimates, however, are owned by the team for two reasons: First, since the team doesn't yet know who will work on the story, ownership of the story cannot be more precisely assigned than to the team collectively. Second, estimates derived by the team, rather than a single individual, are probably more useful.

Since story estimates are owned by the team it is important to have a reasonable portion of the team involved in coming up with the estimates. If the team is large (perhaps seven or more), not every developer needs to be involved, but generally the more developers involved the better. The customer participates while the programmers estimate, but she isn't allowed to contribute her personal estimates or editorialize when she hears an estimate she disapproves of.

Estimating

My preferred estimation approach is derived from the Wideband Delphi approach documented by Boehm (1981). Just like Extreme Programming is an iterative approach to developing software, the approach we'll use to estimating is an iterative approach to developing estimates. Here's how it works:

First, gather together the customer and the developers who will participate in creating the estimates. Bring along the story cards and a stack of additional blank note cards. (Bring some blank cards even if you're maintaining the story descriptions electronically.) Distribute a handful of blank cards to each participant. The customer selects a story at random from the collection and reads it to the developers. The developers ask as many questions as they need and the customer answers them to the best of her ability. If she doesn't know the answer, she takes a guess or asks the team to defer estimating that story.

Everything Takes Four Hours

One of my favorite television shows was *Mad About You*, which is about a recently married couple living in New York. In one episode the husband (Paul Reiser) is being pestered by his wife (Helen Hunt) to go shopping for a couch. She insists the trip will take only an hour. He tells her that "Everything in the world takes four hours. You gotta go there, you gotta do whatever, eat, talk about where you should have eaten, and then come home. That's four hours minimum."

When the programmers estimate a story, they should include everything they'll need to do to complete the story. They need to factor in such things as testing their code, talking to the customer, perhaps helping the customer plan or automate acceptance tests, and so on. If they don't include these activities, it is like they are expecting shopping for a couch to take only an hour.

When there are no more questions about the story, each developer writes an estimate on a card, not yet showing the estimate to the others. If the team has defined a story point as a day of ideal work, the developers think about how many ideal days the story will take to complete. If, instead, the team has defined a story point as, for example, the complexity of the story then the estimate is of the perceived complexity of the story.

When everyone has finished writing an estimate, the estimators turn over their cards or hold them up so everyone can see them. It is very likely at this point that the estimates will differ significantly. This is actually good news. If estimates differ, the high and low estimators explain their estimates. It's important that this does not come across as attacking those estimators. Rather, you want to learn what it is they were thinking about.

As an example, the high estimator may say, "Well, to test this story we're going to need to create a mock database object and that might take us a day. Also, I'm not sure if our standard compression algorithm will work and we may need to write one that is more memory efficient." The low estimator may respond with, "I was thinking we'd store that information in an XML file— that would be easier than a database. Also, I didn't think about needing more data—maybe that will be a problem."

At this point the group discusses it for up to a few minutes. Other estimators will undoubtedly have opinions on whatever reasons the high and low estimators were at the extremes. The customer clarifies issues as they come up. A note or two may be jotted on the story card. Perhaps a new story or two is written.

After the group has discussed the story, the developers again write their estimates on cards. When everyone has written a revised estimate, the cards are again displayed. In many cases the estimates will already converge by the second round. But, if they have not, repeat the process of having the high and low estimators explain the thinking behind their estimates. In many cases the high and low estimators will not be the same as in the first round. In fact, I have sometimes seen cases where the high and low estimators went to opposite extremes after gaining new knowledge during the discussion.

The goal is for the estimators to converge on a single estimate that can be used for the story. It rarely takes more than three rounds, but continue the process as long as estimates are moving closer together. It isn't necessary that everyone in the room turn over a card with exactly the same estimate written down. If I'm involved in an estimation meeting, and on the second round four estimators tell me 4, 4, 4, and 3 story points, I will ask the low estimator if she is OK with a four day estimate. The point is reasonableness not absolute precision. Yes, the developers could probably talk longer and reach consensus on three or four story points, but the time spent doing so isn't worth it.

Triangulate

After the first few estimates have been made, it becomes possible (and necessary) to *triangulate* the estimates. Triangulating an estimate refers to estimating a story based on its relationship to one or more other stories. Suppose a story is estimated at four story points. A second story is estimated at two story points. When the two stories are considered together the programmers should agree that the four-point story is roughly twice the size of the two-point story. Then, when they estimate a story as being three points, they should agree that it is roughly larger than the two-point story yet smaller than the four-point story.

None of this is exact, but triangulation is an effective means for a team to verify that they aren't gradually altering the meaning of a story point. A good way to triangulate is to pin story cards to the wall based on their size. Draw vertical lines on the wall, label each column with the number of story points, and then pin story cards to the wall in the appropriate column, as shown in Figure 8.1. As each new story is estimated, pin it in the appropriate location.

Very quickly compare the newly-estimated story to others in the column to see if it is "about the same."

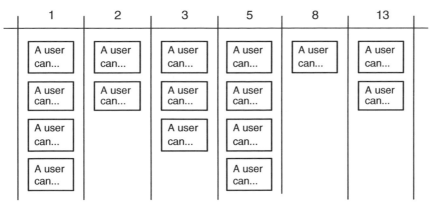

Figure 8.1 *Pin story cards to the wall to facilitate triangulation.*

Using Story Points

At the end of an iteration the team counts the number of story points they completed. They then use that as a forecast of how many story points they'll complete in upcoming iterations of the same length. For example, suppose a team completes 32 story points over a two-week iteration. Our best guess is that they'll also complete 32 story points in the next iteration. We use the term *velocity* to refer to the number of story points a team completes (or expects to complete) in an iteration.

Let's look at how velocity and story points work together and why accuracy isn't important. Suppose a team is starting a new project. They estimate all of the stories for the project and come up with a total of three hundred story points. Before the start of the first iteration they project that collectively they can complete thirty story points per week, which means the project will take ten iterations (weeks).

At the end of the first iteration the team adds up the story points for the stories they completed. They find that rather than completing 30, they completed 50 story points. If they can complete 50 story points in each iteration, they will finish the project in a total of six iterations. Should they plan on maintaining their measured velocity of 50? Yes, they should, based on three conditions.

First, nothing unusual (like a bunch of overtime, an extra programmer, or so on) affected productivity this iteration. The impact of overtime or other productivity factors on velocity is obvious. If velocity of one iteration is based on everyone working sixty-hour weeks, there will be a big drop in velocity in the next iteration if they return to working forty hour weeks.

Second, the estimates need to have been generated in a consistent manner. This is important because it evens out fluctuations in velocity from one iteration to the next. Suppose in one iteration the team worked on nothing but stories that had been estimated only by a notorious overestimator. The team's velocity for that iteration would be artificially high if stories in later iterations were estimated by someone with a different bias. The best way to ensure that estimates are consistent is to use a team estimation process as described in this chapter.

Finally, the stories selected for the first iteration must be independent. This will be the case if stories were written in the manner suggested in Chapter 2, "Writing Stories." Consider an iteration comprised entirely of poorly constructed stories such that all work during the iteration is on the user interface. We would not want to extrapolate the velocity of that iteration onto all remaining iterations.

Why This Works

The Central Limit Theorem tells us that the sum of a number of independent samples from any distribution is approximately normally distributed.

For our purposes, this means that a team's story point estimates can be skewed way toward underestimation, way toward overestimation, or distributed in any other way. But when we grab an iteration's worth of stories from any of those distributions, the stories we grab will be nomally distributed. This means that we can use the measured velocity of one iteration to predict the velocity of future iterations.

Naturally, the velocity of one iteration is not a perfect predictor. For example, an iteration containing one twenty-point story rather than twenty one-point stories would be a less accurate predictor. Similarly, velocity may change as a team learns new technology, a new domain, or becomes accustomed to new team members or new ways of working.

What If We Pair Program?

Whether or not a team chooses to pair program has no effect on story point estimates. For example, suppose a team with two developers is estimating in story points that are based on ideal days of work. They are not pair programming. They plan a one-week iteration that will include two stories, each estimated at three story points. During the iteration they finish those two stories and calculate their team velocity as six.

Suppose instead that they pair program and that they estimate in ideal *pair* days. They look at the stories and decide that each will take two ideal pair days. At the end of the one-week iteration they have completed both stories and calculate their velocity as four.

While represented by different numbers, the velocities in these two cases are the same. The two teams are moving at the same speed since they completed the same amount of work in their iterations. This means that a team can choose to estimate story points in ideal pair days or ideal individual programmer days, and any differences will be reflected in the velocity.

Precision Decreases as Story Size Increases

A problem with estimating in story points is that differences between some numbers can be hard to justify. For example, suppose the developers are considering a story and one developer suggests that the story is worth two story points. Another counters that the story is three story points. This discusson makes sense: three story points represents 50% more work than two story points. It's very possible for two developers to discuss a story and argue about differences of that magnitude.

However, now suppose the developers are arguing over whether a story should be seven or eight story points. In most cases a one point difference between numbers that large is too small to be discussed with any relevance. Arguing about whether a story is worth seven or eight story points implies more precision in our estimation process than we have.

To avoid this situation and simplify things, the team may want to agree to constrain estimates to specific pre-defined values such as:

½, 1, 2, 3, 5, 8, 13, 20, 40, 80

This is appealing because it reflects the truth that as estimates get larger, we know less about them. If the team has an epic to consider they'll have to decide whether it's a 40 or an 80, but they won't have to think about whether it's a 79 or an 80.

Some Reminders

Working with story points can sometimes be confusing. Usually this results from thinking too hard about story points or trying to make them more than they are. To reinforce the ways you can use story points, keep these facts in mind:

- Your team's story points are not equivalent to my team's story points. A story your team estimates as worth three story points may be worth five to my team.

- When a story (possibly an epic) is disaggregated into its constituent stories, the sum of the estimates for the individual stories does not need to equal the estimate of the initial story or epic.

- Similarly, a story may be disaggregated into constituent tasks. The sum of the estimates for the tasks does not need to equal the estimate of the initial story.

Summary

- Estimate stories in story points, which are relative estimates of the complexity, effort or duration of a story.

- Estimating stories needs to be done by the team, and the estimates are owned by the team rather than individuals.

- Triangulate an estimate by comparing it to other estimates.

- Whether or not a team programs in pairs has no impact on story point estimates. Pair programming affects the team's velocity, not their estimates.

Developer Responsibilities

- You are responsible for defining story points in a manner that is relevant and usable by your team. You are responsible for consistently sticking to that definition.

- You are responsible for giving honest estimates. You are responsible for not giving in to temptation or pressure to give low estimates.

- You are responsible for estimating as a team.

- You are responsible for giving estimates that are consistent with other estimates. That is, all the two-point stories should be similar.

Customer Responsibilities

- You are responsible for participating in estimation meetings, but your role is to answer questions and clarify stories. You are not allowed to estimate stories yourself.

Questions

8.1   During an estimating meeting three programmers are estimating a story. Individually they estimate the story at two, four and five story points. Which estimate should they use?

8.2   What is the purpose of triangulating estimates?

8.3   Define velocity.

8.4   Team A finished 43 story points in their last two-week iteration. Team B is working on a separate project and has twice as many developers. They also completed 43 story points in their last two-week iteration. How can that be?

Chapter 9

Planning a Release

Most software projects will do best with a new release every two to six months. Certain website projects may release even more frequently, but even then there is a benefit to collecting related new features into a release. It is frequently useful to start release planning from a product development roadmap showing the main areas of focus for the next handful of new releases. This product development roadmap will certainly change—and we want it to since the changes will be the result of our learning more about our product, its market, and our ability to develop the product.

A product development roadmap can be as simple as a list of the main areas of focus, or *themes* as Kent Beck calls them, for each of the next few releases. For example, for the next release of the BigBucksJobs.com website we may list the following themes:

- resume filtering and screening tools for companies

- automated search agents for job seekers

- improved query performance

Starting with a rough product development roadmap, there are two questions we use to initiate release planning:

- When do we want the release?

- What is the priority of each story?

Once we have the answers to these questions we plan the release by estimating how much work the team will be able to accomplish in each iteration. Using this estimate of how much work we can do in an iteration, we make a reasonable prediction about how many iterations it will take to produce a release that meets the customer's expectations.

When Do We Want the Release?

Ideally, the developers and the customer can talk about a range of dates, rather than a specific date: "We'd like to release in May, but as long as we release sometime in July, that's fine." An iterative, story-driven process makes it easy to fix a date but difficult to fix what will be included by a given date. If a team can start release planning with a range of acceptable dates they will have more flexibility in timing releases. For example, starting with a date range in mind enables a team to make statements like "After six or seven iterations we should have the minimum functionality and maybe ten to twelve before we have everything on the 1.0 wish list."

In some cases the date truly is fixed. Most commonly this occurs when preparing a release for a trade show, a key customer release, or some similar milestone. If this is the case, release planning is actually a bit easier as there are fewer variables to consider. However, the decisions about which stories to include will usually be more difficult.

What Would You Like in It?

In order to plan a release, the customer must prioritize the stories. Prioritizing stories into the familiar high, medium and low categories is useful but can lead to tedious arguments over what constitutes a high priority story as opposed to a medium priority story. Fortunately, we can borrow a technique from DSDM, another of the agile processes.[1]

DSDM includes a prioritization technique referred to as the MoSCoW rules. MoSCoW is an acronym for

- Must have

- Should have

- Could have

- Won't have this time

The must-have features are those that are fundamental to the system. Should-have features are important but there's a short-term workaround for

---

1.   For information on DSDM see *DSDM: Business Focused Development* (Stapleton 2003).

them. If the project has no time constraints, the should-have features would normally be considered mandatory. Could-have features are ones that can be left out of the release if time runs out. Features prioritized as won't-have are ones that are desired but acknowledged as needing to come in a later release.

Prioritizing the Stories

There are many dimensions along which we can sort stories. Among the technical factors we can use are:

- the risk that the story cannot be completed as desired (for example, with desired performance characteristics or with a novel algorithm)

- the impact the story will have on other stories if deferred (we don't want to wait until the last iteration to learn that the application is to be three-tiered and multi-threaded)

Additionally, customers and users have their own set of factors they could use to sort the stories, including the following:

- the desirability of the story to a broad base of users or customers

- the desirability of the story to a small number of important users or customers

- the cohesiveness of the story in relation to other stories (for example, a "zoom out" story may not be high priority on its own but may be treated as such because it is complementary to "zoom in," which is high priority)

Collectively, the developers have a sequence in which they would like to implement the stories, as will the customer. When there is a disagreement to the sequence, the customer wins. Every time.

However, customers cannot prioritize without some information from the development team. Minimally, a customer needs to know approximately how long each story will take. Before the stories are prioritized, they have already been estimated and the estimates written on the story cards, as shown in Story Card 9.1.

At this point the customer does not sum the estimates and make decisions about what will or won't fit in a release. Instead, she uses the estimates, along with her own assessment of the value of each story, to sort the stories so that they maximize the value delivered to the organization. A particular story may be highly valuable to the organization but will take a month to develop. A different story may only be half as valuable but can be developed in a day.

> The site always tells a shopper what the last 3 (?) items she viewed are and provides links back to them. (This works even between sessions.)
>
>
> Estimate: 3 days

■ Story Card 9.1   Provide links back to previously viewed items.

▼──────────────────────────────────▼

Cost Changes Priority

A few years ago my team was building a Windows user interface for a customer who was transitioning a large application from an old DOS-based system. In the DOS system the Enter key was used to move forward between fields. The customer wanted us to do the same in her new Windows system. From her customer perspective it was logical that it would take the same amount of development time to use either Enter or Tab. However, we estimated that it would take about an extra person week to use the Enter key. After hearing that, our customer quickly lowered her priority on that story. It was a high priority to her when she thought it was a few hours; when it was a week, there were many other things she decided she would rather have.

▲──────────────────────────────────▲

Mixed Priorities

If a customer is having trouble prioritizing a story, the story may need to be split. Splitting a story allows the customer to prioritize the separate stories differently. On one project I had the story description shown in Story Card 9.2. The customer struggled to prioritize the story because searching by author and title were essential, while the other search fields were considered nice but were not essential. The story was split into three: one story for searching by author or title, another for searching by publication name or date, and a third allowing for the criteria to be combined.

> Users can search for magazine articles by author, publication name, title, date or any combination of these.

■ Story Card 9.2   Search criteria.

Risky Stories

Looking back over earlier approaches to software development, it is clear that there has been an ongoing debate about whether a project should first go after the riskiest parts or the most valuable parts of the project. Probably the leading proponent of risk-driven development has been Barry Boehm whose spiral model focuses on the early elimination of risk (1988). On the other end has been Tom Gilb who advocates doing the "juicy bits" first (1988).

Agile approaches are firmly in the camp of doing the juicy bits first. This allows agile projects to avoid solving risks too far in advance and allows them to defer building infrastructural code that may not be needed. Favoring the juicy bits also makes it possible for a project to release early, when only the highest-valued functionality is available.

But, even when going after the juicy bits first, we still need to consider risk when prioritizing stories. Many developers have a tendency to want to do the riskiest stories first. Sometimes this is appropriate but the decision must still be made by the customer. However, the customer considers input from the technical team when prioritizing the stories.

On one recent project in the biotech space some of the stories called for novel extensions to a standard statistical approach called expectation maximization. Because the work being undertaken was truly new, the team could not be sure if it could be accomplished at all or how long it would take. The product would still have been saleable without the inclusion of these stories, so the customer prioritized them to be near the middle of the stack. However, once the customer was made aware of the extremely high risk associated with these stories, enough of them were given higher priorities in order to determine what was involved in developing the novel algorithms.

Prioritizing Infrastructural Needs

Frequently the risky stories are associated with infrastructural or nonfunctional needs such as performance. I was on a project to develop a web program that would display charts of stock prices. One of our stories is shown in Story Card 9.3. For the baseline web server machinery that had been specified, this level of performance could be a significant challenge. The difficulty of meeting this performance requirement would have a profound impact on our architectural decisions.

> Be able to generate 50 stock chart images per second.

■ Story Card 9.3   Generate 50 images per second.

We'd already committed to Java as our server-side language but could we achieve 50 images per second with Java? Would we instead need to go with native C or C++ code for the image generation? Or could we achieve our throughput goal with a strong caching algorithm that would serve up the same chart for requests that were only seconds apart?

In this case the customer had written Story Card 9.3 for us. However, she prioritized it fairly low. Our first few iterations would be targeted at developing features that could be shown to prospects and used to generate initial sales and interest in the product. Our customer reasoned that we could always add scalability in later. In some cases it is easy to refactor a system to improve its scalability. In other cases, that type of refactoring can be very difficult. It is up to the developers to help the customer by identifying stories that can be deferred but may become much more costly to develop if implemented later. Developers must not, however, take this as a license to steer the customer toward early implementation of their favorite technical features.

On another project, the customer clearly wanted the application to be deployable as a three–tiered application with a database server, a client machine, and a middle-tier that would route requests and data between them. The customer had talked with the team about this in various meetings and the marketing literature she was preparing described the system as three-tiered. However, none of the stories was written so that it required the addition of the middle tier.

This was becoming troubling to the technical team. They did not mind starting with a simple two-tiered system (database server and client machine) but after a couple of iterations had gone by they became more and more concerned that the middle tier had not been added. They knew that adding the middle tier would still be easy but that it would get a little harder with each iteration. Also, because the user stories were written with their focus entirely on end-user functionality it was not clear when such an infrastructural need would be added.

The solution was to write a story that made the three-tier capability a higher priority to the customer who was prioritizing the team's work. In this case we added the story: "During installation the user can decide to install everything locally on her PC or to install the client, middle-tier and server separately."

Selecting an Iteration Length

Collectively the developers and the customer select an iteration length that will work for them. Iteration lengths are typically from one to four weeks. Short iterations allow for more frequent course corrections of the project and more visibility into its progress; however, there is a slight overhead associated with each iteration. Err on the side of iterations that seem a little too short rather than ones that seem a little too long.

As much as possible, stick with a constant iteration length for the duration of the project. With consistent iterations, projects fall into a natural rhythm that can be beneficial to the pace of the team. Naturally there will be times when you need to alter the iteration length. For example, a team that has been using three-week iterations is asked to prepare the next version for an important tradeshow in eight weeks. Rather than stopping after two three-week iterations with two weeks left before the show, they can start with two normal three-week iterations and then follow those with an abbreviated two-week iteration. There's nothing wrong with this. What you want to avoid is random changes to the iteration length.

From Story Points to Expected Duration

Suppose that the customer has prioritized all of the story cards. The team sums the estimates from each card and comes up with 100 story points. Using story points made it easier for estimating the stories, but now we need a way to convert story points into a predicted duration for the project.

The answer, of course, is to use velocity. As we learned in Chapter 8, "Estimating User Stories," velocity represents the amount of work that gets done in an iteration. Once we know a team's velocity, we can use it to turn ideal days into calendar days. For example, if we estimate our project at 100 ideal days, then with a velocity of 25 we can estimate that it will take 100 / 25 = 4 iterations to complete the project.

The Initial Velocity

There are three ways to get an initial value for velocity:

1. Use historical values.

2. Run an initial iteration and use the velocity of that iteration.

3. Take a guess.

Using historical values is the best option, but it is only viable if we have an existing team that is rolling off a project similar to the new project and if no one is joining or leaving the team. Unfortunately, it is rare that the exact same team gets to work on two consecutive similar projects.

Running an initial iteration is a great way to get a starting velocity. However, there are many times when this is not viable. For example, suppose your boss comes to you with a new product idea. She's written the user stories she thinks are needed in the first version. She's used those stories to do market research and thinks the product will earn $500,000 the first year. If the product can be developed cheaply enough, the company will pursue it. If not, they'll pass. When your boss asks you what it will cost to develop, you are not always given the freedom to say, "Let me run a sample iteration for two weeks and get back to you." In cases like this you need a way to take a guess at the velocity.

Guessing at Velocity

If we need to guess at velocity we should at least do so in a way that makes sense when we explain it to others. Fortunately, there's a reasonable way of doing this if you followed the advice of Chapter 8, "Estimating User Stories," and defined a story point as approximately one ideal day of work.

If a story point is one ideal day of work, we can estimate initial velocity by estimating how many actual days it will take us to complete a full ideal day of work. Over the course of an iteration it is clear the team will have many interruptions that will prevent the team from having ideal days. Their actual days will differ from ideal days because of time spent answering email, phone calls, all-company meetings, departmental meetings, training, giving or attending demos, washing the boss' car, interviewing new candidates, illnesses, vacation, and so on. Because of all of these interruptions it is common to start with an expected velocity that is somewhere between one-third and one-half the number of developer-days in an iteration. For example, a six-person team using two-week (ten working day) iterations would have sixty developer-days each iteration. They may want to estimate velocity between 20 and 30 story points per iteration depending on how different they expect their days to be from ideal days.

Of course, as the project progresses through the first few iterations the team will gain a much better feeling for the duration of the project. They'll know within an iteration or two how far off their velocity estimate was and will be able to refine the estimate and communicate the plan with more confidence.

Creating the Release Plan

So, if the project has 100 story points and we estimate velocity at 20 story points per iteration, then we can expect it to take five iterations. The final step in release planning is to allocate stories into each of the iterations. Collaboratively the customer and the developers select twenty story points worth of the highest priority stories and place them into the first iteration. The next twenty story points go into the second iteration and so on until all the stories have been allocated.

Depending on whether the team is entirely collocated (including stakeholders such as upper managers) and the organization's need for formality, there are many ways to communicate a release plan. For example, I've used each of the following:

- With a collocated team, I've pinned story cards to the wall using columns to indicate the iterations.

- With stories in a spreadsheet, I've sorted the stories based on their iterations and then drawn a thick bold line after the last story in each iteration.

- For interested remote stakeholders, I've photocopied notecards (three to a page, or six to a page if you reduce the size). I indicate the start of each iteration and add a nice cover page.

- For interested, high ceremony, remote stakeholders, I've created trivial Gantt charts. I create entries like "Iteration 1" and then list as subordinate to it the story names for that iteration.

A Warning

Be careful not to put too much faith in the release plan. The techniques described in this chapter will help you estimate the approximate duration of a project and allow you to make statements like "The product will be ready for release in approximately 5–7 iterations." They don't give you enough precision, however, to say things like "We'll be done on June 3."

Use the release plan to set initial expectations but then constantly reset those expectations as you gain new information. Monitor each iteration's velocity and re-estimate the stories whenever you learn something new that affects the estimates.

Summary

- Before planning a release it is necessary to know approximately when the customer would like the release and the relative priorities of the stories.

- Stories should be prioritized into a specific order (first, second, third and so on) rather than into groups (very high, high, medium and so on).

- Stories are prioritized by the customer but with input from the developers.

- Estimates, which are in ideal days, are converted into calendar time using velocity.

- It is often necessary to estimate a team's initial velocity.

Developer Responsibilities

- You are responsible for providing information (sometimes including your underlying assumptions and possible alternatives) to the customer in order to help her prioritize the stories.

- You are responsible for resisting the urge to prioritize infrastructural or architectural needs higher than they should be.

- You are responsible for creating a release plan that is built on realistic estimates yet includes an appropriately sized project buffer.

Customer Responsibilities

- You are responsible for prioritizing the user stories into the precise order you value them. It is not sufficient to sort them into stacks of high, medium and low priority.

- You are responsible for expressing your honest deadlines for the release. If you need it on July 15th, don't tell the developers you need it on June 15th just to be safe.

- You are responsible for understanding the difference between ideal time and calendar time.

- You are responsible for splitting stories that contain components that you want prioritized differently.

- You are responsible for understanding why a programmer with a personal velocity of 0.6 should not be reprimanded or criticized because her velocity is less than 1.0.

Questions

9.1   What are three ways of estimating a team's initial velocity?

9.2   Assuming one-week iterations and a team of four developers, how many iterations will it take the team to complete a project with 27 story points if they have a velocity of 4?

Chapter 10

Planning an Iteration

Release planning has left us with a coarse-grained allocation of stories to the iterations that comprise a release. This level of planning—not so much detail that we give the false feeling of precision and accuracy, but enough planning that we can base actions on it— is ideal for planning a release. However, at the start of each iteration it is important to take the planning process one step further.

Iteration Planning Overview

To plan an iteration the whole team holds an iteration planning meeting. The customer as well as all of the developers (that is, programmers, testers and others) on the team attend and participate in this meeting. Because the team will be looking at the stories in detail, they will undoubtedly have some questions about them. They need the customer present to answer these questions.

The general sequence of activities for an iteration planning meeting is as follows:

1. Discuss a story.

2. Disaggregate the story into its constituent tasks.

3. One developer accepts responsibility for each task.

4. After all stories have been discussed and all tasks have been accepted, developers individually estimate the tasks they've accepted to make sure they are not over-committed.

Each of the activities is discussed in one of the following sections.

Discussing the Stories

As input to the iteration planning meeting, the team has the set of prioritized stories. Just as programmers may change their opinions about the difficulty of programming a story, the customer may change her mind about the priority of a story. The iteration planning meeting is the perfect time for the customer to express these priority changes to the team.

To start the meeting, the customer starts with her highest priority story and reads it to the developers. The developers then ask questions until they understand the story sufficiently to disaggregate it into constituent tasks. It is not necessary to understand every detail of the story, and diving too deeply into the details of each story can make the meeting very lengthy and inefficient, since not everyone in the meeting needs to hear all the detail on all stories. The developers will still be able to work out the fine details of the stories with the customer after the planning meeting.

Changing Priorities

It is usually best if the customer can withstand the desire to change priorities *during* an iteration. It is very easy for a team to get whipsawed during an iteration if the customer changes her mind frequently. On one project, for example, the customer and a programmer met and agreed about how a database search feature would work. Five days into a ten-day iteration (and about two-thirds through coding the search feature), the customer came up with what she thought was a better solution that was completely different from the original, partially coded solution. At that point, in her mind the customer was comparing two uncoded solutions and she naturally favored the one she thought was better. She urged the team to abandon the current approach and immediately start on the new approach. We politely asked her to wait until the end of the iteration and she agreed. At that point, she was comparing a fully working solution that did most of what she wanted in a search feature and another version that was undoubtedly better but that would take 10 days to develop.

Even though she (and the rest of the team) thought the new search feature would be better, it was not worth adding at that point when compared to a fully working adequate feature. Users were better served by having developers work on entirely new features.

Disaggregating into Tasks

There is really no art to disaggregating a story into tasks. Many developers have been doing this for much of their careers. Since stories are already fairly small (typically taking the project's archetypal programmer one to five days of ideal time) there is usually not that much disaggregation necessary.

In fact, why disaggregate at all? Why not leave the story alone as a discrete unit of work?

Even though stories are small enough to serve as units of work, projects are generally well served by disaggregating them into even smaller tasks. First, for many teams the story will not be implemented by just one developer (or one pair of developers). The story may be split among developers either because the developers specialize in certain technologies or because splitting the work is the fastest way to complete the story.

Second, stories are descriptions of user- or customer-valued functionality; they are not to-do lists for developers. The act of converting a story into its constituent tasks is often useful because it helps point out tasks that might have been forgotten. Because the disaggregation into tasks happens in a group setting, the entire strength of the team is brought to the effort. While one developer may forget that it's necessary to update the install program as part of a story, it is less likely that everyone will forget.

One of the criticisms of agile processes is that there is no upfront design step, as there is in a waterfall process. While it's true there is no upfront design *phase*, agile processes are characterized by frequent short bursts of design. Disaggregating stories into tasks—which can only be done with at least a minimal design in mind—is one of these short bursts of just in–time design that replace a waterfall's upfront design phase.

As various team members call out the tasks that comprise a story, someone on the team needs to write the tasks on something. My personal preference is to write them on a white board in a shared team meeting room.

As an example of disaggregating a story into tasks, suppose we have the story "A user can search for a hotel on various fields." That story might be turned into the following tasks:

- code basic search screen

- code advanced search screen

- code results screen

- write and tune SQL to query the database for basic searches

- write and tune SQL to query the database for advanced searches

- document new functionality in help system and user's guide

In particular notice the inclusion of the task for updating the user's guide and help system. Even though this story did not explicitly say anything about documentation, the team knew from prior iterations that there are a help system and a user's guide and that they need to be accurate at the end of each iteration. If there was any question about this the team could have asked the customer.

Guidelines

Because stories are already fairly small it is not necessary to set very precise guidelines around the desired size of a task. Use these guidelines when disaggregating stories into tasks:

- If one task of a story is particularly difficult to estimate (for example, a list of supported data formats requires approval from a remote Vice President who is slow to respond), separate that task from the rest of the story.

- If tasks could easily be done by separate developers, then split those tasks. For example, in the case above, coding of the basic and advanced search screens was separated. There may be some natural synergy to having the same programmer or pair work on both but it isn't necessary. Disaggregating tasks in this way is useful because it lets multiple developers work on the same story. This is frequently necessary near the end of an iteration as time starts to run out. Similarly, the task "code basic search screen" could have been split into two tasks: "Design screen layout for basic search screen" and "Code basic search screen" if the team is using a user interface designer or group.

- If there is benefit in knowing that a part of the story is done, break that part out as a task. In the example above, the coding of the basic and advanced search screens were made separate tasks. This will allow the developer who writes the database access code to connect her SQL to the search screens one at a time as they become available. This means that a delay in the completion of the advanced search screen does not delay completion of the two tasks for the basic search screen.

Accepting Responsibility

Once all the tasks for a story have been identified, someone on the team needs to volunteer to perform each task. If the tasks were written on a white board, developers simply write their names next to the tasks they are accepting.

Even if the team will be doing pair programming, it is generally best to associate a single name with each task. This person assumes responsibility for completing the task. If he needs additional information from the customer, he gets it. If he chooses to pair program, he solicits a pair. Ultimately, though, it is his responsibility to make sure the task gets completed during the iteration.

Actually, it's the responsibility of everyone on the team to make sure the task gets completed. The team needs a "we're all in this together" mentality. And, if near the end of the iteration, one developer is not going to complete all the tasks she accepted, then others on the team are expected to take on that work to the extent possible.

Even though an individual signs up for a task and accepts responsibility for it, these responsibilities must be fluid throughout the iteration. As the team progresses through the iteration, learning more about the tasks, finding some work easier than planned but some harder than planned, commitments need to change. At the end of an iteration no one can say "I finished my work, but Tom still had a few tasks left."

Estimate and Confirm

If a project team's velocity is forty story points per iteration, then the previous steps—discussing a story, disaggregating it into tasks, and accepting responsibility for the tasks—are repeated until the team has discussed the customer's top forty story points worth of stories. At that point each developer is responsible for estimating the amount of work she has accepted responsibility for. The best way to do this is still to estimate in ideal time.

By this point the tasks should be small enough that they can be estimated with some reliability. But, if not, don't worry about it. Take a best guess at the duration of the task and move on. If, as was recommended earlier in this chapter, the tasks and names of the responsible developers were written on a white board, each developer can now add his or her estimates to the board. The result will look something like Table 10.1.

Table 10.1 *It's easy to track tasks, the developer doing each task, and estimates on a white board.*

Task	Who	Estimate
Code basic search screen	Susan	6
Code advanced search screen	Susan	8
Code results screen	Jay	6
Write and tune SQL to query the database for basic searches	Susan	4
Write and tune SQL to query the database for advanced searches	Susan	8
Document new functionality in help system and user's guide	Shannon	2

Once a developer has estimated each of her tasks, she needs to add them up and make a realistic assessment about whether they can all be completed during the iteration. For example, suppose a two-week iteration is beginning and I have accepted tasks that I now estimate will take 53 hours of actual time on task. It's doubtful that with everything else I have to do that I will be able to put that much time directly onto these tasks. At this point I have the following options:

- keep all the tasks and hope

- request that someone else on the team take some of my tasks

- talk with the customer about dropping a story (or splitting a story and dropping part of it)

If one of the developers finishes assessing her workload and feels she can take on my tasks, responsibility for them can move to her. If, however, no one has any additonal capacity to take on the tasks, then the customer has to help by removing some work from the iteration. Each developer must feel comfortable committing to the work she's signed up for. And, since the team has a "we're all in this together" attitude, everyone needs to be comfortable with the overall commitment of the team.

Summary

- Iteration planning takes release planning one step further but only for the iteration being started.

- To plan the iteration, the team discusses each story and disaggregates it into its constituent tasks.

- There is no mandatory size range for tasks (for example, three to five hours). Instead, stories are disaggregated into tasks to facilitate estimation or to encourage more than one developer to work on various parts of the story.

- One developer accepts responsibility for each task.

- Developers assess whether they have over-committed themselves by estimating each task they have accepted.

Developer Responsibilities

- You are responsible for participating in the iteration planning meeting.

- You are responsible for helping to disaggregate all stories into tasks, not just the stories you are likely to work on.

- You are responsible for accepting responsibility for the tasks you will work on.

- You are responsible for ensuring you take on an appropriate amount of work.

- Throughout an iteration you are responsible for monitoring the amount of work you have left as well as the amount of work your teammates have left. If you're likely to finish your work, you are responsible for taking on some work from your teammates.

Customer Responsibilities

- You are responsible for prioritizing the stories that will be included in the iteration.

- You are responsible for directing the developers toward the greatest business value they can deliver. This means that if higher-value stories have come to light since the release plan was first established, you are responsible for adjusting priorities to deliver maximum business value.

- You are responsible for participating in the iteration planning meeting.

Questions

10.1 Disaggregate this story into its constituent tasks: A user can view detailed information about a hotel.

Chapter 11

Measuring and Monitoring Velocity

As you recall from Chapter 9, "Planning a Release," the release plan was created by breaking the project into a series of iterations, where each iteration included a certain number of story points. The number of story points completed in an iteration is known as the project's velocity. When planning the project, we either used a known velocity (if we had one, perhaps from another similar project) or we made one up. Velocity can be a useful management tool, so it is important to look at the team's velocity at the end of each iteration as well as during the iterations.

Measuring Velocity

Because velocity can be such an important measure, it is important to think about how we'll measure it. Most stories are easy to count: The team completed them during the iteration so they are counted at full value. Assume, for example, that a team completed the stories shown in Table 11.1 during an iteration. As can be seen in this table, the team's velocity is 23, which is the sum of the story points for the stories completed in the iteration. If the release plan assumed a velocity that is significantly different from 23, it may be necessary to reconsider the project plan. However, be careful about adjusting a release plan too early. Not only is an initial velocity prone to error, it can also be very volatile during early iterations. You may want to wait two or three iterations until you have a longer-term view of velocity.

117

Table 11.1 *Stories completed during an iteration.*

Story	Story Points
A user can...	4
A user can...	3
A user can...	5
A user can...	3
A user can...	2
A user can...	4
A user can...	2
Velocity	**23**

But, what about stories the team only partially completed? Should they be included in velocity calculations?

No, you should not include partially completed stories when calculating velocity. There are a number of reasons why. First, there's the natural difficulty of figuring out what percentage of a story is complete. Second, we don't want to imply a false precision to velocity by reporting it with fractional values like 43.8. Third, incomplete stories do not typically represent anything of value to users or customers. So, even though they may have been partially coded, such stories are often left out of formal end-of-iteration builds if the software is to be delivered to any users. Fourth, if stories are so big that including a partial story routinely affects velocity, say from 41 to 50, then the stories are too large. Finally, we desperately want to avoid a situation where many stories are 90% done, yet few are 100% done. A great deal of complexity can lurk in that last 10%, so it is important to finish each story completely before counting it.

If you find yourself tempted to include partially complete stories, evaluate the size of your average story and consider striving for smaller stories. At the end of an iteration when determining velocity, it is far easier to forego half of a one-point story than it is to ignore a twelve-point story. Additionally, if you frequently find iterations finishing with many partially complete stories (even if they are all half-point stories), this may be a symptom of a lack of teamwork on the team. With an all–for–one approach the team will learn they are better off joining together to complete some stories, leaving others unstarted, than they are partially completing all of them.

Velocity Does Not Use Actual Hours

Notice that velocity calculations are made using the story point values assigned before the start of the iteration. Once the iteration is complete, do not change the points the team earns for any story in the iteration. For example, suppose a story was estimated to be four story points but was much larger. After the fact, the team acknowledges they should have estimated it at seven points. This story contrbutes four points to the velocity calculation, not seven.

In general, teams are encouraged to plan the velocity of the next iteration to be no more than the velocity of the prior iteration. However, if the team is truly convinced that a story was estimated too low and they can do more in the upcoming iteration, then they should be allowed to plan on a slightly higher velocity.

While a team cannot retroactively change the points of a completed story, they should always make use of this type of information in adjusting the estimates of any future stories.

Planned and Actual Velocity

A good way to monitor whether actual velocity is deviating from planned velocity—and, more importantly, whether it's something you need to act on—is to graph planned and actual velocity for each iteration. This can be seen in Figure 11.1, which shows planned velocity starting low but then increasing and stabilizing by the third iteration.

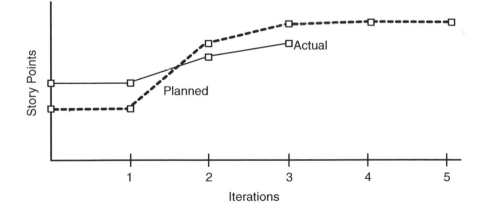

Figure 11.1 *Planned and actual velocity after the first three iterations.*

Actual velocity, graphed through the third iteration, exceeded planned velocity for the first iteration. However, the actual improvements during the second and third iterations were not as great as planned and so actual velocity is slightly less than planned velocity.

The team of Figure 11.1 would have been wrong if, at the conclusion of the first iteration, they told the customer they were exceeding planned velocity and could move up the delivery date. What about after the three iterations shown? Can the team tell if they should adjust the customer's expectations about the release plan? To answer that question the team needs both the velocity graph of Figure 11.1 as well as the cumulative story point graph of Figure 11.2.

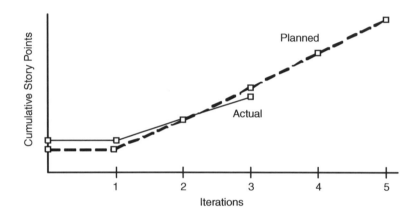

Figure 11.2 *Plotting cumulative planned and actual story points.*

The cumulative story point chart shows the total number of story points completed through the end of each iteration. So, we can see in Figure 11.2 that through the end of the second iteration the team had completed more story points than planned, even though progress in the second iteration was much slower than planned. However, by the end of the third iteration, the advantage of the team's good start in the first iteration has been eroded by slower progress during the second and third iterations.

By the end of the third iteration it appears probable that the team will not complete as much functionality as planned. If the customer is not aware of this from daily interaction with the team, the situation should be made clear to her.

Iteration Burndown Charts

Another useful way of looking at progress is through the use of an *iteration burndown chart*. An iteration burndown chart shows the amount of work, expressed in story points, remaining at the end of each iteration. An example is shown in Figure 11.3.

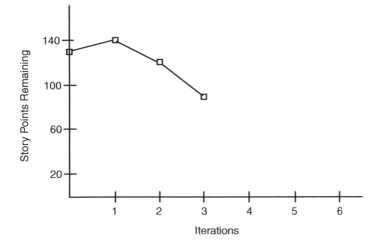

Figure 11.3 *An iteration burndown chart.*

An interesting feature of a burndown chart is that it reflects both progress made in the form of story points completed, as well as changes to the number of story points planned for the remainder of the release. For example, suppose a team completes twenty story points during an iteration, but the customer adds fifteen story points worth of new work to the project. The twenty story points reflects a net gain of only five; if the developers are working optimally then the customer may have to slow the introduction of new work if she expects the project to be finished quickly.

Figure 11.3 shows a team that actually had negative overall progress during the first iteration. They started the first iteration with 115 story points to complete and ended the iteration with 120. Managers and customers need to be careful that they don't read a burndown chart like Figure 11.3 and go yell at the team. What we can't tell from a burndown chart is how fast the team is moving. The team on Figure 11.3 may have completed 90 story points, but the customer may have added 95. To know how many story points the team is completing, look at a velocity chart (like the one shown in Figure 11.1) or a cumulative story point chart (like the one shown in Figure 11.2).

Burndown charts are useful—even though they don't show the speed of the development team—because they present a better overall view of the project's progress. A strength of agile software development is that a project can begin without a lengthy upfront complete specification of the project's requirements. Agile teams acknowledge that it is impossible for customers to know everything in advance. So, agile teams instead ask customers to tell them as much as they can and allow customers to change or refine their opinions as the project progresses, and everyone learns more about the software being built. This means that stories will come and go, that stories will change size, and that stories will change in importance. As an example of this, consider the project shown in Table 11.2.

Table 11.2 *Progress and changes during four iterations.*

	Iteration 1	Iteration 2	Iteration 3	Iteration 4
Story points at start of iteration	130	113	78	31
Completed during iteration	45	47	48	31
Changed estimates	10	4	–3	
Story points from new stories	18	8	4	
Story points at end of iteration	113	78	31	0

The team on this project thought they could do around 45 story points each iteration. They started with 130 story points and a plan to run for three iterations. They completed exactly 45 story points in the first iteration. But, in completing those stories, they decided that a few of the remaining stories were bigger than initially thought and they increased the estimates on the unstarted stories by ten story points. Additionally, the customer wrote six new stories, each of which was estimated to be three story points. This means that while the team completed 45 story points, their net progress is 45–10–18, or 17 story points. This means that at the end of the first iteration they have 113 story points remaining. At this point the team could tell they would not finish in three iterations as planned. Even if no new stories came in, they had more than the 90 story points remaining, the amount they could reasonably expect to finish in the remaining two iterations. The customer and team met and considered stopping after three iterations—leaving some functionality out of the software—but, instead they agreed to let the project run for four iterations.

The second iteration followed a similar trend as the first, with the team completing 47 story points but increasing estimates of unstarted stories by 4 points. The customer slowed the pace of change but still added new stories worth 8 story points. Net progress during the second iteration was 47–4–8=35 story points.

The team started the third iteration with 78 story points left. Things went well and the team completed stories worth 48 story points. They also reduced estimates of unstarted stories by three story points. (Remember that in the previous two iterations, estimates of unstarted work had gone up.) The customer added a story or two worth a total of four story points. Net progress during the third iteration was 48+3–4=47. This left only 31 story points for the fourth iteration, which the team completed without any further changes.

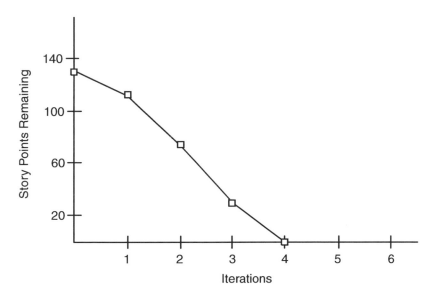

Figure 11.4 *Burndown chart for the project in Table 11.2.*

A burndown chart for this project is shown in Figure 11.4. As you can see from this chart, it was obvious from the slope of the burndown line after the first iteration that the project would not be finished after three iterations.

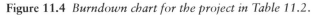

Burndown Charts During an Iteration

Beyond their usefulness for tracking progress at the end of iterations, burndown charts are also a great management tool during the iteration. During an iteration, a *daily burndown chart* shows the estimated number of hours left in the iteration. For example, see Figure 11.5, which shows a daily tracking of the hours remaining in an iteration.

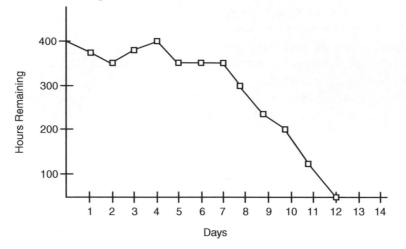

Figure 11.5 *A daily burndown chart.*

I prefer to collect information on the remaining level of effort by having each team member adjust his hours remaining on a common whiteboard. When iteration planning is done, the notes are left on the whiteboard that was used. At that point the board will contain a list of stories with each story disaggregated into one or more tasks. Next to each task is a place for the programmer to sign up for the tasks. About once a day I add up the numbers on the whiteboard and add them to a burndown chart for the iteration. Near the start of an iteration, a portion of such a whiteboard will look similar to Figure 11.6.

Create HTML page	Thad	2̶	0
Read search fields from HTML form	Thad	2	
Create better sample data	Mary	2̶	4
Write servlet to perform search	Mary	4	
Generate results page	Thad	2	

Figure 11.6 *Estimates are written, and frequently revised, on a whiteboard.*

Figure 11.6 shows that the task "Create HTML page" has been completed as its estimate of remaining work has gone from two hours to none. However, Mary has increased her estimate for the "Create better sample data" task. It doesn't matter whether Mary hasn't started but changed her mind, or whether she's already spent two (or four or six) hours on it and thinks there are four to go. All that matters is that the estimate on the board reflects her current thinking about how much work is left.

Everyone on the team knows to keep the numbers relatively current. It usually works best if the board is updated whenever a task is finished or at the end of the day. This way everything is always relatively current. Everyone on the team needs to be encouraged to have the estimates of remaining work be as accurate as possible. Programmers need to feel equally comfortable increasing an estimate of time remaining as they do decreasing it.

Hours Remaining, Not Hours Expended

Notice that daily burndown charts reflect the amount of work remaining, not the amount of work expended on a story or task. There may be a few good reasons for tracking hours expended (such as to compare actual to planned effort to improve estimating skills, or to monitor the number of productive hours spent each week). However, these are outweighed by the reasons not to capture hours expended (such as the feeling of being micromanaged most developers will feel and the effort or imprecision in the numbers).

Besides, what really matters is how much effort is left, not how much effort has been applied so far.

Naturally, new tasks can be added, too. However, a new task should be added only when someone realizes that a task was forgotten and the forgotten task is necessary for the completion of a story already included in the current iteration. New tasks should not be added just because someone wants something new included in the iteration; that type of change needs to be prioritized into an iteration at the next planning session.

▼───▼

Use Big, Visible Charts

All of the charts shown in this chapter are most useful when made big and visible. If your organization has a plotter then print the charts on the plotter and hang them on a wall in the team's common area or in a commonly used hallway. If you don't have a plotter, think about hanging a few large whiteboards on a wall and usng those to draw the charts.

At one location we hung three large, four-foot by six-foot whiteboards in a common area. I got some small black tape at a stationery store and used it to draw axes on the whiteboards. This gave us permanently straight axes that weren't erased when we changed the chart. Each week we'd add a point to each of the three charts. Periodically, we'd run out of space so we'd erase the chart and start over.

▲───▲

Summary

- When determining velocity count only finished stories, that is, stories that pass their acceptance tests. Do not count stories the team partially completed during the iteration.

- A good way to monitor differences between actual and planned velocity is to graph both the number of story points planned and those actually completed for each iteration.

- Don't try to predict trends in velocity after only one or two iterations.

- The number of actual hours spent completing a task or a story have no bearing on velocity.

- Post big, visible charts in common areas where everyone can see them.

- A cumulative story point chart (as shown in Figure 11.2) is useful because it shows the the total number of story points completed through the end of each iteration.

- An iteration burndown chart (as shown in Figure 11.3) shows both progress in the form of story points completed as well as changes to the number of story points planned for the remainder of the release.

- A daily burndown chart, showing the hours left on each day of an iteration, is very useful during an iteration.

- Charting and watching a team's defects per story point helps indicate if increases in velocity are coming at the expense of defects.

Developer Responsibilities

- To the extent possible, you are responsible for completing one story before moving onto the next story. It is preferable to have a small number of completed stories than to have a slightly larger number of stories all incomplete.

- You are responsible for understanding the impact of any decision you make on the velocity of the project.

- You are responsible for understanding how to read and interpret each of the charts shown in this chapter.

- If you are a manager or perhaps in the Tracker role on an XP project, you are responsible for knowing how and when to create the charts shown in this chapter.

Customer Responsibilities

- You are responsible for understanding how to read and interpret each of the charts shown in this chapter.

- You are responsible for knowing the velocity of the team.

- You are responsible for knowing how actual velocity compares to the planned velocity and whether plan corrections are needed.

- You are responsible for adding or removing stories from the release to ensure that the objectives of the project are met to the extent possible given its constraints.

Questions

11.1   A story estimated at one story point actually took two days to complete. How much does it contribute to velocity when calculated at the end of the iteration?

11.2   What can you learn from a daily burndown chart that you can't see on an iteration burndown chart?

11.3   What conclusions should you draw from Figure 11.7? Does the project look like it will finish ahead, behind or on schedule?

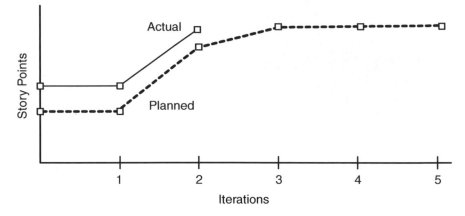

Figure 11.7 *Will this project finish ahead, behind or on schedule?*

11.4   What is the velocity of the team that finished the iteration shown in Table 11.3?

Table 11.3 *Stories completed during an iteration.*

Story	Story Points	Status
Story 1	4	Finished
Story 2	3	Finished
Story 3	5	Finished
Story 4	3	Half finished
Story 5	2	Finished
Story 6	4	Not started
Story 7	2	Finished
Velocity	23	

11.5   What circumstances would cause an iteration burndown chart to reflect an upward trend?

11.6   Complete Table 11.4 by writing the missing values into the table.

Table 11.4 *Fill in the missing values.*

	Iteration 1	Iteration 2	Iteration 3
Story points at start of iteration	100		
Completed during iteration	35	40	36
Changed estimates	5	−5	0
Story points from new stories	6	3	
Story points at end of iteration	76		0

PART III

Frequently Discussed Topics

We've looked at what stories are, how we can use them, and how we can estimate and plan using them. In Part III we start by turning our attention to how stories differ from other requirements approaches such as requirements specification documents, scenarios, and use cases. Next we look at the advantages user stories have over these other approaches.

As with any approach, however, things can sometimes go wrong and our attention turns next to a list of smells, or indicators that something may be amiss. User stories originated in, and are most closely associated with, Extreme Programming. In Part III we will see how user stories can be added to Scrum, another of the agile processes. Part III concludes with a discussion of some additional smaller but frequently discussed topics such as whether stories should be written on paper or stored electronically, whether stories should be written for bugs, and so on.

Chapter 12

What Stories Are Not

To help us better understand what user stories are, it's important to look at what they are not. This chapter explains how user stories differ from three other common approaches to requirements: use cases, IEEE 830 software requirements specifications, and interaction design scenarios.

User Stories Aren't IEEE 830

The Computer Society of the Institute of Electrical and Electronics Engineers (IEEE) has published a set of guidelines on how to write software requirements specifications (IEEE 1998). This document, known as IEEE Standard 830, was last revised in 1998. The IEEE recommendations cover such topics as how to organize the requirements specification document, the role of prototyping, and the characteristics of good requirements. The most distinguishing characteristic of an IEEE 830-style software requirements specification is the use of the phrase "The system shall..." which is the IEEE's recommended way to write functional requirements. A typical fragment of an IEEE 830 specification looks similar to the following:

4.6)   The system shall allow a company to pay for a job posting with a credit card.
    4.6.1)   The system shall accept Visa, MasterCard and American Express cards.
    4.6.2)   The system shall charge the credit card before the job posting is placed on the site.
    4.6.3)   The system shall give the user a unique confirmation number.

Documenting a system's requirements to this level is tedious, error-prone, and very time-consuming. Additionally, a requirements document written in this way is, quite frankly, boring to read. Just because something is boring to read is not sufficient reason to abandon it as a technique. However, if you're dealing with 300 pages of requirements like this (and that would only be a medium-sized system), you have to assume that it is not going to be thoroughly read by everyone who needs to read it. Readers will either skim or skip sections out of boredom. Additionally, a document written at this level will frequently make it impossible for a reader to grasp the big picture.

A Warning Sign

One warning sign of a project going astray with a requirements specification is a ping-ponging of the specification document between the software development group and another group like Marketing or Product Management. What typically happens is the Product Management (or similar) group writes a requirements specification that is given to the developers. The developers then rewrite this document so that it conveys their interpretation of the requirements as first written by Product Management. The developers are always careful to give their document a completely different name (something like Functional Specification perhaps) to hide that it is the same document as the initial document, just written from the perspective of a different group.

Both groups know that a requirements specification for a project of any significance is too difficult to read and fully understand and impossible to write with the desired precision. So, whichever group writes the final requirements can claim ownership of the intent of the document. When the project is finished and blame is being allocated they will point to sections of the document and claim that missing features were implied. Or they will claim that expected functionality is clearly out of scope because of a sentence buried somewhere in the document.

Most of the times when I see two groups writing separate versions of essentially the same document I already know they are positioning themselves for the end-of-project blame sessions and for claiming to know the intent of the document. This type of silliness goes away with user stories. Along with the shift to conversations from documentation comes the freedom of knowing that nothing is final. Documents that look like contracts feel so final. Conversations don't feel that way. If we talk today and then learn something next month, we talk again.

There is a tremendous appeal to the idea that we can think, think, think about a planned system and then write all the requirements as "The system shall…" That sounds so much better than "if possible, the system will…" or even "if we have time, we'll try to…" that better characterizes the reality on most projects.

Unfortunately, it is effectively impossible to write all of a system's requirements this way. There is a powerful and important feedback loop that occurs when users see the software being built for them. When users see the software, they will come up with new ideas and change their minds about old ideas. When changes are requested to the software described in a requirements specification, we've become accustomed to calling it a "change of scope." This type of thinking is incorrect for two reasons. First, it implies that the software was at some point sufficiently well-known for its scope to have been considered fully defined. It doesn't matter how much effort is put into upfront thinking about requirements, we've learned that users will have different (and better) opinions once they see the software. Second, this type of thinking reinforces the belief that software is complete when it fulfills a list of requirements, rather than when it fulfills its intended users' goals. If the scope of the user's goals changes then perhaps we can speak of a "change of scope," but the term is usually applied even when it is only the details of a specific software solution that have changed.

IEEE 830-style requirements have sent many projects astray because they focus attention on a checklist of requirements rather than on the user's goals. Lists of requirements do not give the reader the same overall understanding of a product that stories do. It is very difficult to read a list of requirements without automatically considering solutions in your head as you read. Carroll (2000) suggests that designers "may produce a solution for only the first few requirements they encounter." For example, consider the following requirements:[1]

3.4)   The product shall have a gasoline-powered engine.
3.5)   The product shall have four wheels.
    3.5.1)   The product shall have a rubber tire mounted to each wheel.
3.6)   The product shall have a steering wheel.
3.7)   The product shall have a steel body.

By this point I suppose images of an automobile are floating around your head. Of course, an automobile satisfies all of the requirements listed above. The one in your head may be a bright red convertible while I might be envisioning a blue pickup. Presumably the differences between your convertible and my pickup are covered in additional requirements statements.

But suppose that instead of writing an IEEE 830-style requirements specification, the user told us her goals for the product:

- The product makes it easy and fast for me to mow my lawn

- I am comfortable while using the product

---

1.   Adapted from *The Inmates Are Running the Asylum* (Cooper 1999).

By looking at the user's goals, we get a completely different view of the product and realize that the customer really wants a riding lawn mower, not an automobile. These goals are not user stories, but where IEEE 830 documents are a list of requirements, stories describe a user's goals. By focusing on the user's goals for the new product, rather than a list of attributes of the new product, we are able to design a better solution to the user's needs.

A final difference between user stories and IEEE 830-style requirements specifications is that with the latter the cost of each requirement is not made visible until all the requirements are written down. The typical scenario is that one or more analysts spends two or three months (often longer) writing a lengthy requirements document. This is then handed to the programmers who tell the analysts (who relay the message to the customer) that the project will take twenty-four months, rather than the six months they had hoped for. In this case, time was wasted writing the three-fourths of the document that the team won't have time to develop, and more time will be wasted as the developers, analysts and customer iterate over which functionality can be developed in time. With stories, an estimate is associated with each story right up front. The customer knows the velocity of the team and the story point cost of each story. After writing enough stories to fill all the iterations, she knows she's done.

Kent Beck explains this difference with an analogy of registering for a wedding.[2] When you register for a wedding you don't see the cost of each item. You just make a wish list of everything you want. That may work for weddings, but it doesn't work for software development. When a customer places an item on her project wish list, she needs to know the cost of it.

How and Why Will the Feature Be Used?

A further problem with requirements lists is that the items on the lists describe the behavior of the software, not the behavior or goals of a user. A requirements list rarely answers "But how and why will someone use this feature?"

Steve Berczuk, XP developer and author of *Software Configuration Management Patterns*, points out the importance of this question: "I can't count the number of times that I saved a whole lot of work by taking a feature list and asking a customer to create scenarios that use those features. Often the customer will realize that the feature really isn't needed, and that you should spend time building things that add value."[3]

2.   Personal communication, November 7, 2003.
3.   Steve Berczuk on extremeprogramming@yahoogroups.com, February 20, 2003.

User Stories Are Not Use Cases

First introduced by Ivar Jacobsen (1992), use cases are today most commonly associated with the Unified Process. A use case is a generalized description of a set of interactions between the system and one or more actors, where an actor is either a user or another system. Use cases may be written in unstructured text or to conform with a structured template. The templates proposed by Alistair Cockburn (2001) are among the most commonly used. A sample is shown in Figure 12.1, which is equivalent to the user story "A Recruiter can pay for a job posting with a credit card."

Since this is not a book on use cases we won't fully cover all the details of the use case shown in Figure 12.1; however, it is worth reviewing the meaning of the Main Success Scenario and Extensions sections. The Main Success Scenario is a description of the primary successful path through the use case. In this case, success is achieved after completing the five steps shown. The Extensions section defines alternative paths through the use case. Often, extensions are used for error handling; but, extensions are also used to describe successful but secondary paths, such as in extension 3a of Figure 12.1. Each path through a use case is referred to as a *scenario*. So, just as the Main Success Scenario represents the sequence of steps one through five, an alternate scenario is represented by the sequence 1, 2, 2a, 2a1, 2, 3, 4, 5.

One of the most obvious differences between stories and use cases is their scope. Both are sized to deliver business value, but stories are kept smaller in scope because we place constraints on their size (such as no more than ten days of development work) so that they may be used in scheduling work. A use case almost always covers a much larger scope than a story. For example, looking at the user story "A Recruiter can pay for a job posting with a credit card" we see it is similar to the main success scenario of Figure 12.1. This leads to the observation that a user story is similar to a single scenario of a use case. Each story is not necessarily equivalent to a main success scenario; for example, we could write the story "When a user tries to use an expired credit card the system prompts her to enter a different credit card," which is equivalent to Extension 2b of Figure 12.1.

User stories and use cases also differ in the level of completeness. James Grenning has noted that the text on a story card "plus acceptance tests are basically the same thing as a use case."[4] By this Grenning means that the story cor-

---

4. James Grenning on extremeprogramming@yahoogroups.com, February 23, 2003.

> **Use Case Title:** Pay for a job posting
>
> **Primary Actor:** Recruiter
>
> **Level:** Actor goal
>
> **Precondition:** The job information has been entered but is not viewable.
>
> **Minimal Guarantees:** None
>
> **Success Guarantees:** Job is posted; recruiter's credit card is charged.
>
> **Main Success Scenario:**
>
> 1. Recruiter submits credit card number, date, and authentication information.
> 2. System validates credit card.
> 3. System charges credit card full amount.
> 4. Job posting is made viewable to Job Seekers.
> 5. Recruiter is given a unique confirmation number.
>
> **Extensions:**
>
> 2a: The card is not of a type accepted by the system:
>
> > 2a1: The system notifies the user to use a different card.
>
> 2b: The card is expired:
>
> > 2b1: The system notifies the user to use a different card.
>
> 2c: The card is expired:
>
> > 2c1: The system notifies the user to use a different card.
>
> 3a: The card has insufficient available credit to post the ad.
>
> > 3a1: The system charges as much as it can to the current credit card.
> >
> > 3a2: The user is told about the problem and asked to enter a second credit card for the remaining charge. The use case continues at Step 2.

Figure 12.1 *A sample use case for pay for a job posting.*

responds to the use case's main success scenario, and that the story's tests correspond to the extensions of the use case.

For example, in Chapter 6, "Acceptance Testing User Stories," we saw that appropriate acceptance test cases for the story "A Recruiter can pay for a job posting with a credit card" might be:

- Test with Visa, MasterCard and American Express (pass).

- Test with Diner's Club (fail).

- Test with good, bad and missing card ID numbers.

- Test with expired cards.

- Test with different purchase amounts (including one over the card's limit).

Looking at these acceptance tests we can see the correlation between them and the extensions of Figure 12.1.

Another important difference between use cases and stories is their longevity. Use cases are often permanent artifacts that continue to exist as long as the product is under active development or maintenance. Stories, on the other hand, are not intended to outlive the iteration in which they are added to the software. While it is possible to archive story cards, many teams simply rip them up.

An additional difference is that use cases are more prone to including details of the user interface, despite admonishments to avoid this (Cockburn 2001; Adolph, Bramble, et al. 2002). There are several reasons this happens. First, use cases often lead to a large volume of paper and without another suitable place to put user interface requirements they end up in the use cases. Second, use case writers focus too early on the software implementation rather than on business goals.

Including user interface details causes definite problems, especially early on in a new project when user interface design should not be made more difficult by preconceptions. I recently came across the use case shown in Figure 12.2, which describes the steps for composing and sending an email message.

Use Case Title: Compose and send email message
Main Success Scenario:
1. User selects the "New Message" menu item.
2. System presents the user with the "Compose New Message" dialog.
3. User edits email body, subject field and recipient lines.
4. User clicks the Send button.
5. System sends the message.

Figure 12.2 *A use case to compose and send an email message.*

This use case has user interface assumptions throughout. It assumes that there is a "New Message" menu item, that there is a dialog for composing new messages, that there are subject and recipient input fields on that dialog, and that there is a Send button. Many of these assumptions may seem good and safe but they may rule out a user interface where I click on a recipient's name to initiate the message instead of typing it in. Additionally, the use case of Figure 12.2 precludes the use of voice recognition as the interface to the system.

Admittedly, there are far more email clients that work with typed messages than with voice recognition, but the point is that a use case is not the proper place to specify the user interface like this. Think about the user story that would replace Figure 12.2: "A user can compose and send email messages." No hidden user interface assumptions there. With stories, the user interface will come up during the conversation with the customer.

To get around the problem of user interface assumptions in use cases, Constantine and Lockwood (1999) have suggested the use of *essential use cases*. An essential use case is a use case that has been stripped of hidden assumptions about technology and implementation details. For example, Table 12.1 shows an essential use case for composing and sending an email message. What is interesting about essential use cases is that the user intentions could be directly interpreted as user stories.

Another difference is that use cases and stories are written for different purposes (Davies 2001). Use cases are written in a format acceptable to both customers and developers so that each may read and agree to them. Their purpose is to document an agreement between the customer and the development team. Stories, on the other hand, are written to facilitate release and iteration planning, and to serve as placeholders for conversations about the users' detailed needs.

Table 12.1 *An essential use case.*

User Intention	System Responsibility
Compose email message	
Indicate recipient(s)	
	Collect email content and recipient(s)
Send email message	
	Send the message

Not all use cases are written by filling in a form, as shown in Figure 12.1. Some use cases are written as unstrucutred text. Cockburn refers to these as *use case briefs*. Use case briefs differ from user stories in two ways. First, since a use case brief must still cover the same scope as a use case, the scope of a use case brief is usually larger than the scope of a user story. That is, one use case brief will typically tell more than one story. Second, use case briefs are intended to live on for the life of a product. User stories, on the other hand, are disposed of.

Finally, use cases are generally written as the result of an analysis activity, while user stories are written as notes that can be used to initiate analysis conversations.

User Stories Aren't Scenarios

In addition to referring to a single path through a use case, the word *scenario* is also used by human-computer interaction designers. In this context a scenario is a detailed description of a user's interaction with a computer. The scenarios of interaction design are not the same as a scenario of a use case. In fact, an interaction design scenario is typically larger, or more encompassing, than even a use case. For example, consider this scenario:

> Maria is thinking about making a career change. Since the glory days of the dot-com boom she has worked as a tester at Big-TechCo. A former high school math teacher, Maria decides she'll be happier if she returns to teaching. Maria goes to the BigMoney-Jobs.com website. She creates a new account with a user name and password. She then creates her resume. She wants to find a job as a math teacher anywhere in Idaho but preferably near her current job in Coeur d'Alene. Maria finds a handful of jobs that match her search criteria. The job that intrigues her most is with the North Shore School, a private high school in Boise. Maria has a friend, Jessica, in Boise whom she hopes may know someone at North Shore. Maria enters Jessica's email address and forwards the job link to her with a note asking if she knows anyone at the school. The next morning Maria gets an email from Jessica saying that she doesn't know anyone at the school, but she knows of the North Shore School and it has a wonderful reputation. Maria clicks on a button that submits her resume to North Shore.

Carroll (2000) says that scenarios include the following characteristic elements:

- a setting
- actors
- goals or objectives
- actions and events

The setting is the location where the story takes place. In the story about Maria the story presumably takes place on her home computer; but since that is not stated, the location of the story could be her office during the workday.

Each scenario includes at least one actor. It is possible for a scenario to have multiple actors. For example, in our scenario both Maria and Jessica are actors. Maria may be referred to as the *primary actor* because the scenario mostly describes her interactions with the system. However, because Jessica receives an email from the system and then uses the website to look at the job posting, she is considered a *secondary actor*. Unlike use cases, actors in interaction design scenarios are always people and never other systems.

Each actor in a scenario is pursuing one or more goals. As with actors, there can be primary and secondary goals. For example, Maria's primary goal is to find an appropriate job in her desired location. While working to achieve that goal, she pursues secondary goals such as viewing detailed information about a hotel or sharing information with a friend.

Carroll refers to the actions and events as the *plot* of a scenario. They are the steps an actor takes to achieve her goal or a system's response. Searching for a job in Idaho is an action Maria performs. The response to that action is the event of the system displaying a list of matching jobs.

The primary differences between user stories and scenarios are scope and detail. Scenarios contain much more detail and their scope usually covers multiple stories. The example scenario contains many possible stories, such as:

- a user can send information about a job to a friend via email

- a user can create a resume

- a user can submit her resume for a matching job

- a user can search for a job by geographic region

Even with their additional detail, scenarios (like stories) leave details to be worked through in a discussion. For example:

- Maria logged onto the site with a user name and password. Are all users required to log onto the site? Or does logging on enable some of the features Maria used (perhaps the feature to send an email)?

- When Jessica receives the email, does the email contain information about the job or does it just link to a page on the site with that information?

Summary

- User stories are different from IEEE 830 software requirements specifications, use cases and interaction design scenarios.

- No matter how much thinking, thinking and thinking we do, we cannot fully and perfectly specify a non-trivial system upfront.

- There is a valuable feedback loop that occurs between defining requirements and users having early and frequent access to the software.

- It is more important to think about users' goals than to list the attributes of a solution.

- User stories are similar to a use case scenario. But use cases still tend to be larger than a single story and can be more prone to containing embedded assumptions about the user interface.

- Additionally, user stories differ from use cases in their completeness and longevity. Use cases are much more complete than are user stories. Use cases are designed to be permanent artifacts of the development process; user stories are more transient and not intended to outlive the iteration in which they are developed.

- User stories and use cases are written for different purposes. Use cases are written so that developers and customers can discuss them and agree to them. User stories are written to facilitate release planning and to serve as reminders to fill in requirements details with conversations.

- Unlike IEEE 830 specifications and use cases, user stories are not artifacts of analysis activities. Rather, user stories are a support tool for analysis.

- Interaction design scenarios are much more detailed than user stories and differ in the kind of detail provided.

- A typical interaction design scenario is much larger than a user story. One scenario may comprise multiple use cases, which, in turn, may comprise many user stories.

Questions

12.1   What are the key differences between user stories and use cases?

12.2   What are the key differences between user stories and IEEE 830 requirements statements?

12.3   What are the key differences between user stories and interaction design scenarios?

12.4   For a non-trivial project, why is it impossible to write all the requirements at the start of the project?

12.5   What is the advantage to thinking about users' goals rather than on listing the attributes of the software to be built?

Chapter 13

Why User Stories?

With all of the available methods for considering requirements, why should we choose user stories? This chapter looks at the following advantages of user stories over alternative approaches:

- User stories emphasize verbal communication.

- User stories are comprehensible by everyone.

- User stories are the right size for planning.

- User stories work for iterative development.

- User stories encourage deferring detail.

- User stories support opportunistic design.

- User stories encourage participatory design.

- User stories build up tacit knowledge.

After having considered the advantages of user stories over alternative approaches, the chapter concludes by pointing out a few potential drawbacks to user stories.

Verbal Communication

Humans used to have such a marvelous oral tradition; myths and history were passed orally from one generation to the next. Until an Athenian ruler started writing down Homer's *The Iliad* so that it would not be forgotten, stories like Homer's were told, not read. Our memories must have been a lot better back then and must have started to fade sometime in the 1970s because by then we could no longer remember even short statements like "The system shall prompt the user for a login name and password." So, we started writing them down.

And that's where we started to go wrong. We shifted focus to a shared document and away from a shared understanding.

It seems so easy to think that if everything is written down and agreed to then there can be no disagreements, developers will know exactly what to build, testers will know exactly how to test it, and, most importantly, customers will get exactly what they wanted. Well, no, that's wrong: Customers will get the developers' interpretation of what was *written down,* which may not be exactly what they *wanted.*

Until trying it, it would seem simple enough to write down a bunch of software requirements and have a team of developers build exactly what you want. However, if we have trouble writing a lunch menu with sufficient precision, think how hard it must be to write software requirements. At lunch the other day my menu read:

> Entrée comes with choice of soup or salad and bread.

That should not have been a difficult sentence to understand but it was. Which of these did it mean I could choose?

> Soup or (Salad and Bread)
> (Soup or Salad) and Bread

We often act as though written words are precise, yet they aren't. Contrast the words written on that menu with the waitress' spoken words: "Would you like soup or salad?" Even better, she removed all ambiguity by placing a basket of bread on the table before she took my order.

Just as bad is that words can take on multiple meanings. As an extreme example, consider these two sentences:

> Buffalo buffalo buffalo.
> Buffalo buffalo Buffalo buffalo.

Wow. What can those sentences possibly mean? Buffalo can mean either the large furry animal (also known as a bison), or a city in New York, or it can mean "intimidate," as in "The developers were buffaloed into promising an earlier delivery date." So, the first sentences means that bison intimidate other bison. The second sentence means that bison intimidate bison from the city of Buffalo.

Unless we're writing software for bison this is an admittedly unlikely example; but is it really much worse than this typical requirements statement:

- The system should prominently display a warning message whenever the user enters invalid data.

Does *should* mean the requirement can be ignored if we want? I *should* eat three servings of vegetables a day; I don't. What does *prominently display* mean? What's prominent to whoever wrote this may not be prominent to whoever codes and tests it.

As another example, I recently came across this requirement that was referring to a user's ability to name a folder in a data management system:

- The user can enter a name. It can be 127 characters.

From this statement it is not clear if the user must enter a name for the folder. Perhaps a default name is provided for the folder. The second sentence is almost completely meaningless. Can the folder name be another length or must it always be 127 characters?

Writing things down does have advantages: written words help overcome the limitations of short-term memory, distractions, and interruptions. But, so many sources of confusion—whether from the imprecision of written words or from words with multiple meanings—go away if we shift the focus from writing requirements down to talking about them.

Naturally, some of the problems of our language exist with verbal as well as with written communication; but when customers, developers and users talk there is the opportunity for a short feedback loop that leads to mutual learning and understanding. With conversations there is not the false appearance of precision and accuracy that there is with written words. No one signs off on a conversation and no one points to it and says, "Right there, three months ago on a Tuesday, you said passwords could not contain numbers."

Our goal with user stories is not to document every last detail about a desired feature; rather, it is to write down a few short placeholding sentences that will remind developers and customers to hold future conversations. Many of my conversations occur through email and I couldn't possibly do my job without it. I send and receive hundreds of emails every day. But, when I need to talk to someone about something complicated, I invariably pick up the phone or walk to the person's office or workspace.

A recent conference on traditional requirements engineering included a half-day tutorial on writing "perfect requirements" and promised to teach techniques for writing better sentences to achieve perfect requirements. Writing *perfect* requirements seems like such a lofty and unattainable goal.

And even if each sentence in a requirements document is perfect, there are still two problems. First, users will refine their opinions as they learn more about the software being developed. Second, there is no guarantee that the sum of these perfect parts is a perfect whole. Tom Poppendieck has reminded me that 100 perfect left shoes does not yield a single perfect pair of shoes. A far more valuable goal than perfect requirements is to augment *adequate stories* with *frequent conversations*.

User Stories Are Comprehensible

One of the advantages that use cases and scenarios bring us over IEEE 830-style software requirements specifications is that they are understandable by both users and developers. IEEE 830-style documents often contain too much technical jargon to be readable by users and too much domain-specific jargon to be readable by developers.

Stories take this further and are even more comprehensible than use cases or scenarios. Constantine and Lockwood (1999) have observed that the emphasis scenarios place on realism and detail can cause scenarios to obscure broader issues. This makes it more difficult when working with scenarios to understand the basic nature of the interactions. Because stories are terse and are always written to show customer or user value, they are always readily comprehensible by business people and developers.

Additionally, a study in the late 1970s found that people are better able to remember events if they are organized into stories (Bower, Black and Turner 1979). Even better, study participants had better recall of both stated actions as well as inferred actions. That is, not only do stories facilitate recall of stated actions, they facilitate recall of the unstated actions. The stories we write can be more terse than traditional requirements specifications or even use cases, and because they are written and discussed as stories, recall will be greater.

User Stories Are the Right Size for Planning

Additionally, user stories are the right size for planning—not too big, not too small, but just right. At some point in the career of most developers it has been necessary to ask a customer or user to prioritize IEEE 830-style requirements. The usual result is something like 90% of the requirements are mandatory, 5% are very desirable but can be deferred briefly, and another 5% may be deferred a bit longer. This is because it's hard to prioritize and work with thousands of sentences all starting with "The system shall..." For example, consider the following sample requirements:

4.6)   The system shall allow a room to be reserved with a credit card.

    4.6.1)   The system shall accept Visa, MasterCard and American Express cards.

        4.6.1.1)   The system shall verify that the card has not expired.

    4.6.2)   The system shall charge the credit card the indicated rate for all nights of the stay before the reservation is confirmed.

4.7)   The system shall give the user a unique confirmation number.

Each level of nesting within an IEEE 830 requirements specification indicates a relationship between the requirements statements. In the example above, it is unrealistic to think that a customer could prioritize 4.6.1.1 separately from 4.6.1. If items cannot be prioritized or developed separately, perhaps they shouldn't be written as separate items. If they are only written separately so that each may be discretely tested, it would be better to just write the tests directly.

When you consider the thousands or tens of thousands of statements in a software requirements specification (and the relationships between them) for a typical product, it is easy to see the inherent difficulty in prioritizing them.

Use cases and interaction design scenarios suffer from the opposite problem—they're just too big. Prioritizing a few dozen use cases or scenarios is sometimes easy but the results are often not useful because it is rarely the case that all of the top priority items are more important than all of the second priority items. Many projects have tried to correct this by writing many smaller use cases with the result that they swing too far in that direction.

Stories, on the other hand, are of a manageable size such that they may be conveniently used for planning releases, and by developers for programming and testing.

User Stories Work for Iterative Development

User stories also have the tremendous advantage that they are compatible with iterative development. I do not need to write all of my stories before I begin coding the first. I can write some stories, code and test those stories, and then repeat as often as necessary. When writing stories I can write them at whatever level of detail is appropriate. Stories work well for iterative development because of how easy it is to iterate over the stories themselves.

For example, if I'm just starting to think about a project, I may write epic stories like "the user can compose and send email." That may be just right for very early planning. Later I'll split that story into perhaps a dozen other stories:

- A user can compose an email message.

- A user can include graphics in email messages.

- A user can send email messages.

- A user can schedule an email to be sent at a specific time.

Scenarios and IEEE 830 documents do not lend themselves to this type of progressive levels of detail. By the way they are written, IEEE 830 documents imply that if there is no statement saying "The system shall…" then it is assumed that the system shall not. This makes it impossible to know if a requirement is missing or simply has not been written yet.

The power of scenarios is in their detail. So, the idea of starting a scenario without detail and then progressively adding detail as it is needed by the developers makes no sense and would strip scenarios of their usefulness entirely.

Use cases can be written at varying progressive levels of detail, and Cockburn (2001) has suggested excellent ways of doing so. However, rather than writing use cases with free-form text, most organizations define a standard template. The organization then mandates that all use cases conform to the template. This becomes a problem when many people feel compelled to fill in each space on a form. Fowler (1997) refers to this as *completism*. In practice, few organizations are able to write some use cases at a summary level and some at a detailed level. User stories work well for completists because—so far—no one has proposed a template of fields to be written for each story.

Stories Encourage Deferring Detail

Stories also have the advantage that they encourage the team to defer collecting details. An initial place-holding goal-level story ("A Recruiter can post a new job opening") can be written and then replaced with more details once it becomes important to have the details.

This makes user stories perfect for time-constrained projects. A team can very quickly write a few dozen stories to give them an overall feel for the system. They can then plunge into the details on a few of the stories and can be coding much sooner than a team that feels compelled to complete an IEEE 830-style software requirements specification.

Stories Support Opportunistic Development

It is tempting to believe that we can write down all of the requirements for a system and then think our way to a solution in a top-down manner. Nearly two decades ago Parnas and Clements (1986) told us that we will never see a project work this way, because:

- Users and customers do not generally know exactly what they want.

- Even if the software developers know all the requirements, many of the details they need to develop the software become clear only as they develop the system.

- Even if all the details could be known up front, humans are incapable of comprehending that many details.

- Even if we could understand all the details, product and project changes occur.

- People make mistakes.

If we can't build software in a strictly top-down manner, then how do we build software? Guindon (1990) studied how software developers think about problems. She presented a small set of software developers with a problem in designing an elevator control system for a building. She then videotaped and observed the developers as they worked through the problem. What she found was that the developers did not follow a top-down approach at all. Rather, the developers followed an *opportunistic* approach in which they moved freely between considering the requirements to inventing and discussing usage scenarios, to designing at various levels of abstraction. As the developers perceived opportunities to benefit from shifting their thinking between, they readily did so.

Stories acknowledge and overcome the problems raised by Parnas and Clements. Through their heavy reliance on conversation and their ability to be easily written and rewritten at varying levels of detail, stories provide a solution:

- that is not reliant on users fully knowing and communicating their exact needs in advance

- that is not reliant on developers being able to fully comprehend a vast array of details

- that embraces change

In this sense, stories acknowledge that software must be developed opportunistically. Since there can be no process that proceeds in a strictly linear path from high-level requirements to code, user stories easily allow a team to shift between high- and low-levels of thinking and talking about requirements.

User Stories Encourage Participatory Design

Stories, like scenarios, are engaging. Shifting the focus from talking about the attributes of a system to stories about users' goals for using the system leads to more interesting discussions about the system. Many projects have failed because of a lack of user participation; stories are an easy way to engage users as participants in the design of their software.

In *participatory design* (Kuhn and Muller 1993; Schuler and Namioka 1993) the users of a system become a part of the team designing the behavior of their software. They do not become a part of the team through management edict ("Thou shalt form a cross-functional team and include the users"); rather, the users become part of the team because they are so engaged by the requirements and design techniques in use. In participatory design, for example, users assist in the prototyping of the user interface from the beginning. They are not involved only after an initial prototype is available for viewing.

Standing in contrast to participatory design is *empirical design*, in which the designers of new software make decisions by studying the prospective users and the situations in which the software will be used. Empirical design relies heavily on interview and observation but users do not become true participants in the design of the software.

Because user stories and scenarios are completely void of technical jargon, they are totally comprehensible to users and customers. While well-written use cases may avoid technical jargon, readers of use cases must typically learn how to interpret the format of the use cases. Very few first-time readers of a use case have an implicit understanding of common fields on use case forms such as extensions, preconditions and guarantees. Typical IEEE 830 documents suffer from both the inclusion of technical jargon and from the inherent difficulty of comprehending a lengthy, hierarchically-organized document.

The greater accessibility of stories and scenarios encourages users to become participants in the design of the software. Further, as users learn how to characterize their needs in stories that are directly useful to developers, developers more actively engage the users. This virtuous cycle benefits everyone involved in developing or using the software.

Stories Build Up Tacit Knowledge

Because of the emphasis placed on face-to-face communication, stories promote the accumulation of tacit knowledge across the team. The more often developers and customers talk to each other and among themselves, the more knowledge builds up within the team.

Why Not Stories?

Having looked at a number of reasons why stories are a preferred approach to agile requirements, let's also consider their drawbacks.

One problem with user stories is that, on a large project with many stories, it can be difficult to understand the relationships between stories. This problem can be lessened by using roles and by keeping stories at a moderate to high level until the team is ready to start developing the stories. Use cases have an inherent hierarchy that helps when working with a large number of requirements. A single use-case, through its main success scenario and extensions, can collect the equivalent of many user stories into a single entity.

A second problem with user stories is that you may need to augment them with additional documentation if requirements traceability is mandated of your development process. Fortunately, this can usually be done in a very lightweight manner. For example, on one project where we were doing subcontracted development to a much larger, ISO 9001-certified company, we were required to demonstrate traceability from requirements to tests. We achieved this in a very light manner: At the start of each iteration we produced a document that contained each story we planned to do in the iteration. As tests were developed, the test names were added to the document. During the iteration we kept the document up to date by adding or removing stories that moved into or out of the iteration. This addition to our process probably cost us an hour a month.

Finally, while stories are fantastic at enhancing tacit knowledge within a team, they may not scale well to extremely large teams. Some communication on large teams simply must be written down or the information does not get dispersed among as many on the team. However, keep in mind the very real tradeoff between a large number of people knowing a little (through written, low-bandwidth documents) and a smaller number of people knowing a lot (through high-bandwidth face–to–face conversations).

Summary

- User stories force a shift to verbal communication. Unlike other requirements techniques that rely entirely on written documents, user stories place significant value on conversations between developers and users.

- The shift toward verbal communicate provides rapid feedback cycles, which leads to greater understanding.

- User stories are comprehensible by both developers and users. IEEE 830 software requirements specifications tend to be filled with too much technical or business jargon.

- User stories, which are typically smaller in scope than use cases and scenarios but larger than IEEE 830 statements, are the right size for planning. Planning, as well as programming and testing, can be completed with stories without further aggregation or disaggregation.

- User stories work well with iterative development because it is easy to start with an epic story and later split it into multiple smaller user stories.

- User stories encourage deferring details. Individual user stories may be written very quickly, and it is also extremely easy to write stories of different sizes. Areas of less importance, or that won't be developed initially, may easily be left as epics, while other stories are written with more detail.

- Stories encourage opportunistic development, in which the team readily shifts focus between high and low levels of detail as opportunities are discovered.

- Stories enhance the level of tacit knowledge on the team.

- User stories encourage participatory, rather than empirical, design, in which users become active and valued participants in designing the behavior of the software.

- While there are many reasons to use stories, they do have some drawbacks: on large projects it can be difficult to keep hundreds or thousands of stories organized; they may need to be augmented with additional documents for traceability; and, while great at improving tacit knowledge through face–to–face communication, conversations do not scale adequately to entirely replace written documents on large projects.

Developer Responsibilities

- You are responsible for understanding why you have chosen any technique you choose. If the project team decides to write user stories, you are responsible for knowing why.

- You are responsible for knowing the advantages of other requirements tecniques or for knowing when it may be appropriate to apply one. For example, if you are working with a customer and cannot come to an understanding about a feature, perhaps discussing an interaction design scenario or developing a use case may help.

Customer Responsibilities

- One of the biggest advantages of user stories over other requirements approaches is that they encourage participatory design. You are responsible for becoming an active participant in designing what your software will do.

Questions

13.1   What are four good reasons for using user stories to express requirements?

13.2   What can be two drawbacks to using user stories?

13.3   What is the key difference between participatory and empirical design?

13.4   What is wrong with the requirements statement, "All multipage reports should be numbered"?

Chapter 14

A Catalog of Story Smells

This chapter will present a catalog of "bad smells," that is, indicators that something is amiss in a project's application of user stories. Each smell will be described and one or more solutions provided.

Stories Are Too Small

Symptom: A frequent need to revise estimates.

Discussion: Small stories often cause problems with the estimating and scheduling of stories. This happens because the estimate assigned to a small story can change dramatically depending on the order in which the story is implemented. For example, consider these two small stories:

- Search results may be saved to an XML file.

- Search results may be saved to an HTML file.

There is clearly a great deal of overlapping work between these two stories. Time spent on one of the stories will reduce the time spent on the other. Stories like these should be combined for planning purposes. When the story is slotted into an iteration the story can be split; but, until it is necessary, the stories should remain combined.

Interdependent Stories

Symptom: Difficulty planning iterations because of dependencies between stories.

Discussion: When two or more stories are dependent upon one another, it becomes difficult to plan the individual stories into iterations. The team finds itself in a situation where a particular story may only be added to an iteration if

157

another story is also added to the iteration. But that story may only be added if a third story is also added, and so on. This is caused when stories are either too small or have been inappropriately split.

If you suspect that stories are too small, the easy solution is to simply combine the interdependent stories into one. If, instead, the stories appear for all other purposes to be appropriately sized, then look at how the interdependent stories have been separated. Chapter 7, "Guidelines for Good Stories," offered the suggestion that stories be split so as to be a full "slice of cake," including functionality from all layers of the application.

Goldplating

Symptom: Developers are adding features that were not planned for the iteration, or are interpreting stories liberally and going beyond what is necessary to implement a story.

Discussion: *Goldplating* refers to the addition of unnecessary features by the developers. Some developers have a tendency to add enhancements or to go beyond what is needed to satisfy a customer's stated needs. This can happen for a couple of reasons. First, some developers like "wowing" the customer and that is harder to do with the greater customer involvement in agile processes. If the customer is involved day–to–day it is hard to give her a pleasant surprise and get the "wow" some developers enjoy.

Second, when working on agile, story-driven projects with short iterations, developers typically feel a great deal of pressure to always be producing. Goldplating allows them a brief chance to escape this pressure. After all, if the feature can't be finished in time, no one will even know it had been started.

Finally, developers enjoy putting their own mark on a project, and adding a few pet features is one way for them to do this.

An Example of Goldplating

On one project I was on we had a story to take a very crowded screen and rewrite it as a tabbed dialog to improve usability. After the developer finished this change, he enhanced the low-level tab dialog code in this application so that a tab could be torn from its current location and moved about the screen. This was not something the customer asked for. Developers need to stay focused on the stories prioritized by the customer. If a developer has a good idea for a new story, she should suggest it to the customer for possible inclusion in the next iteration.

If a project is experiencing significant goldplating by developers, it can be prevented by increasing the visibility of the tasks that everyone is working on. For example, hold brief daily meetings where everyone says what he or she is working on. With greater visibility into what each developer is working on the team will self-police against gold-plating.

Similarly, end–of–iteration review meetings where all of the new functionality is demonstrated in detail for the customer and other stakeholders will help identify goldplating that occurred during the iteration. It will be too late to correct it during that iteration but the team will be more aware of it for future iterations.

Finally, if the project has a QA organization they can also help identify goldplating, especially if they were involved in the conversations between the programmer and the customer.

Too Many Details

Symptom: Too much time is being spent gathering details well in advance of a story being implemented. Or, more time is spent writing about stories than talking about them.

Discussion: One of the benefits to writing stories on notecards is that the space available for writing the story is quite limited. It is hard to cram lots of detail onto a small card. Including too many details in a story is indicative of placing too much value on documentation and favoring it over conversation.

Tom Poppendieck (2003) has made the observation that "If you run out of room, use a *smaller* card." This is a great idea because it forces story writers to very consciously include fewer details in the stories.

Including User Interface Detail Too Soon

Symptom: Stories written early in a project (especially a project to develop a new product) that include detail about the user interface.

Discussion: At some point on a project the team will definitely write user stories with very direct assumptions (or even direct knowledge) about the user interface. For example, "A Job Seeker can view information about the hiring company from the Job Description page." However, for as long as possible you should avoid writing stories with this level of detail.

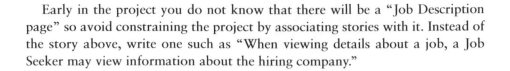

Early in the project you do not know that there will be a "Job Description page" so avoid constraining the project by associating stories with it. Instead of the story above, write one such as "When viewing details about a job, a Job Seeker may view information about the hiring company."

Thinking Too Far Ahead

Symptom: Indicators of this smell may be that stories are hard to fit on note cards, there is interest in using a software system instead of note cards that isn't driven by team size or location, someone proposes a story template to capture all of the details necessary for a story, or perhaps that a suggestion is made to give estimates in finer precision (for example, hours instead of days).

Discussion: This smell is particularly common among teams accustomed to large upfront "requirements engineering" efforts. For a team to overcome this smell they may need a refresher course on the strengths of stories. Fundamental to the use of stories is the recognition that for most problems it is impossible to identify all requirements in advance. Good software emerges through repeated iterations in which increasing amounts of detail are added to the software. Stories fit well with this approach because of the ease with which detail can be expressed in later versions of a story. The team may need to remind itself what it was about their prior development process that led them to adopt stories.

Splitting Too Many Stories

Symptom: Frequently splitting stories during iteration planning so that the right amount of work fits in the iteration.

Discussion: When the developers and customer select the stories they will move into an iteration, they will sometimes need to split a story into two or more constituent stories. Typically a story needs to be split during planning for one of two reasons:

1. The story is too large to fit into the iteration.

2. The story contains both high and low sub-stories, and the customer only wants the high priority sub-stories done during the coming iteration.

Neither of these cases is representative of a problem. Many projects and teams will have occasions when it will be useful to split a story to accommodate the duration of a sprint and fit with the team's observed velocity. However, the situation begins to smell when the team finds itself splitting stories frequently.

If stories are being split more often than feels reasonable, then consider taking a pass through the remaining stories and looking for stories that should be split.

Customer Has Trouble Prioritizing

Symptom: Choosing among and prioritizing stories is often difficult; but sometimes prioritizing the stories is so difficult that it can be considered a smell.

Discussion: If a customer is having trouble prioritizing stories, the first thing to consider is the size of the stories. If stories are too large, they can be difficult to prioritize. Suppose, at the extreme, the BigMoneyJobs website included only the following three stories:

- A Job Seeker can search for jobs.

- A Company can post a job opening.

- A Recruiter can search for candidates.

Pity the poor customer who has to prioritize only among these stories! Her reaction is probably to say, "But can't I have a little of this and some of that?" In this case, get rid of the current stories and replace them with smaller ones so that she can select the pieces of each that she wants.

Also, it may be difficult to prioritize stories if they have not been written to express business value. For example, suppose the customer is presented with these stories:

- A user connects to the database via a connection pool.

- A user can view detailed error information in a log file.

Stories like these can be very difficult for the customer to prioritize because the business value of each is not clear. The stories should be rewritten so that the value of each is clear to the customer. How each is rewritten will vary depending on the customer's technical knowledge, which is why the best recommendation is to have the customer write the stories herself. For example, consider these rewritten versions of the preceding stories:

- A user can start the application without a noticeable lag while connecting to the database.

- Whenever an error occurs, users are given enough information to know how to correct the error.

Customer Won't Write and Prioritize the Stories

Symptom: The customer on a project will not accept responsibility for writing or prioritizing the stories.

Discussion: In a blame-filled organization there are always some individuals who have learned that their best decision is to avoid all responsibility. If you're not responsible for something you can't be blamed for it when it fails, yet there's usually a way to lay claim to at least some of the success. Individuals in this type of culture will want nothing to do with hard decisions like prioritizing features into and out of releases. They'll fall back on statements such as "It's not my problem that you can't complete everything by the deadline, figure out a way to do it."

The best solution I've found in these situations is to find a way to let the customer off the hook. I find a non-threatening way for her to express her opinions. Depending on the individual, this may have to be a private conversation. If I'm working with multiple customers, I tell them each that I'm collecting input from others but that I'm the one who will be responsible for the final decisions, especially if they turn out to be wrong.

Summary

In this chapter we learned about the following smells:

- stories that are too small

- interdependent stories

- goldplating

- adding too many details to stories

- including user interface details too soon

- thinking too far ahead

- splitting too many stories
- trouble when prioritizing stories
- customer won't write and prioritize stories

Developer Responsibilities

- You share a responsibility with the customer to be aware of these smells—as well as any others you may detect—and then to work to correct any that affect your project.

Customer Responsibilities

- You share a responsibility with the developers to be aware of these smells—as well as any others you may detect—and then to work to correct any that affect your project.

Questions

14.1   What should you do if the team is consistently finding it difficult to plan the next iteration?

14.2   What should the team do if they are consistently running out of room to write on the story cards?

14.3   What could cause the customer to have a difficult time prioritizing stories?

14.4   How do you know if you are splitting too many stories?

Chapter 15

Using Stories with Scrum

User stories originated as part of Extreme Programming. Naturally, stories fit perfectly with the other practices of Extreme Programming. However, stories also work well as the requirements approach for other processes.

In this chapter we'll look at Scrum, another agile process, and will see how stories can be integrated as an important part of Scrum.[1] Terms that are part of the Scrum lexicon will be italicized when first used.

Scrum Is Iterative and Incremental

Like XP, Scrum is both an iterative and an incremental process. Since these words are used so frequently without definition, we'll define them.

An iterative process is one that makes progress through successive refinement. A development team takes a first cut at a system, knowing it is incomplete or weak in some (perhaps many) areas. They then iteratively refine those areas until the product is satisfactory. With each iteration the software is improved through the addition of greater detail. For example, in a first iteration a search screen might be coded to support only the simplest type of search. The second iteration might add additional search criteria. Finally, a third iteration may add error handling.

A good analogy is sculpting. First the sculptor selects a stone of the appropriate size. Next the sculptor carves the general shape from the stone. At this point one can perhaps distinguish the head and torso, and discern that the finished work will be of a human body rather than a bird. Next, the sculptor refines her work by adding detail. However, the sculptor is unlikely to look on any one area as complete until the entire work is complete.

---

1. For complete coverage of Scrum, see *Agile Development with Scrum* (Schwaber and Beedle 2002).

An incremental process is one in which software is built and delivered in pieces. Each piece, or increment, represents a complete subset of functionality. The increment may be either small or large, perhaps ranging from just a system's login screen on the small end to a highly flexible set of data management screens. Each increment is fully coded and tested, and the common expectation is that the work of an iteration will not need to be revisited.

An incremental sculptor would pick one part of her work and focus entirely on it until it's finished. She may select small increments (first the nose, then the eyes, then the mouth, and so on) or large increments (head, torso, legs and then arms). However, regardless of the increment size, the incremental sculptor would attempt to finish the work of that increment as completely as possible.

Scrum and XP are both incremental and iterative. They are iterative in that they plan for the work of one iteration to be improved upon in subsequent iterations. They are incremental because completed work is delivered throughout the project.

The Basics of Scrum

Scrum projects progress through a series of thirty-day iterations called *sprints*. At the start of each sprint the team determines the amount of work it can accomplish during that sprint. Work is selected from a prioritized list called the *product backlog*. The work the team believes it can complete during the sprint is moved onto a list called the *sprint backlog*. A brief daily meeting, the *daily scrum*, is held to allow the team to inspect its progress and to adapt as necessary. Graphically, Scrum is as shown in Figure 15.1, which is adapted from Ken Schwaber's website at www.controlchaos.com.

The Scrum Team

A Scrum team typically consists of four to seven developers. While a Scrum team may involve specialist developers—testers and database administrators, for example—a Scrum team shares a "we're all in this together" attitude. If there is testing to be done and there is no dedicated tester available, then someone else does the testing. All work is owned collectively. Scrum teams are self-organizing. That is, there is no management directive stating that Mary codes and Bill tests. Because of this, role names such as programmer, architect and tester are generally not used on Scrum teams. Everything about how a team accomplishes its work is left up to the team.

This core team is supplemented by two key people: the *product owner* and the *ScrumMaster*. A Scrum product owner is essentially the customer of Extreme Programming. The product owner is largely responsible for placing items onto and prioritizing the product backlog list of needed functionality. The ScrumMaster is similar to a project manager except that the role is much more one of leadership than of managing. Because Scrum teams are self-organizing and given great leeway in how they complete the work of a sprint, the project's ScrumMaster serves the team rather than directs it. A ScrumMaster typically serves her team by removing obstacles to progress and by helping the team follow the few simple rules of Scrum.

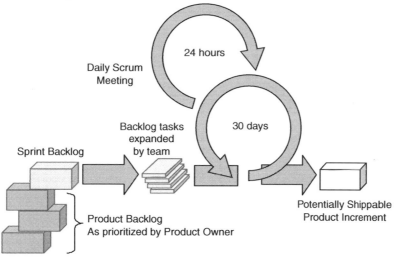

Figure 15.1 *Graphical representation of the Scrum process.*

The Product Backlog

The product backlog is the master list of all functionality desired in the product. When a project is initiated there is no comprehensive effort to write down all foreseeable features. Typically, the product owner and team write down everything obvious, which is almost always more than enough for a first sprint. The product backlog is then allowed to grow and change as more is learned about the product and its customers.

An example product backlog from a real project appears as shown in Table 15.1. As you can see from this table, backlog items can be technical tasks ("Refactor the Login class to throw an exception") or more user-centric ("Allow undo on the setup screen").

The product owner sorts the product backlog into priority order. Even better, the product owner is allowed (actually encouraged) to shuffle the product backlog items as priorities change from month to month.

Table 15.1 *A sample product backlog list.*

Number	Description
1	Finish database versioning
2	Get rid of unneeded Java in the database
3	Refactor the Login class to throw an exception
4	Add support for concurrent user licensing
5	Add support for evaluation licenses
6	Support wildcards when searching
7	Save user settings
8	Allow undo on the setup screen

The Sprint Planning Meeting

A *sprint planning meeting* is held at the start of each sprint. The meeting usually lasts up to a full day and is attended by the product owner, the ScrumMaster and the entire team of developers. Also attending may be any interested and appropriate management or customer representatives.

During the first half of the sprint planning meeting, the product owner describes the highest priority remaining features to the team. The team asks enough questions that during the second half of the meeting they can determine which items they will move from the product backlog to the sprint backlog.

The product owner does not have to describe every item being tracked on the product backlog. Depending on the size of the backlog and the velocity of the team it may be sufficient to describe only the high priority items, saving the discussion of lower priority items for the next sprint planning meeting. Typically, the Scrum team will provide guidance when they start to get further into the backlog list than they know can be done in the upcoming sprint.

Collectively the team and the product owner define a *sprint goal*, which is a short description of what the team plans to achieve during that sprint. In a *sprint review meeting* held at the end of the sprint, the team will assess their success against the sprint goal, rather than against each specific item selected from the product backlog.

During the second half of the sprint planning meeting, the team meets separately to discuss what they heard and decide how much they can commit to during the coming sprint. Conceptually, the team starts at the top of the prioritized product backlog list and draws a line after the lowest of the high priority tasks they feel they can complete. In practice it is not unusual to see a team select, for example, the top five items and then two items from lower on the list that are associated with the initial five. In some cases there will be negotiation with the product owner, but it will always be up to the team to determine how much they can commit to completing.

The Main Rules of Scrum

A sprint planning meeting is held at the start of each sprint.

Each sprint must deliver working and fully tested code that demonstrates something of value to end-users or the customer.

The product owner prioritizes the product backlog.

The team collectively selects the amount of work brought into the sprint.

Once a sprint begins, only the team may add to the sprint backlog.

The product backlog may be added to or reprioritized at any time.

A short scrum meeting is held every day. Each project participant answers: What did you do yesterday? What will you do today? What obstacles are in your way?

Only active participants in the sprint (not interested observers or removed stakeholders) may speak during the daily scrum meeting.

The result of a sprint is demonstrated at a sprint review meeting at the end of the sprint.

Working software is demonstrated during the sprint review. No slideshows are allowed.

No more than two hours may be spent preparing for the sprint review.

Once the sprint starts, only the team may add work to the sprint. The CEO cannot approach the team and ask for something the product owner left out. A salesperson cannot ask for one more feature for a special customer. And the product owner cannot change her mind and ask for additional features. The only time work may be added to a sprint is if the team finds itself ahead of schedule. At that time the team can ask the product owner to help identify an additional item or two.

In exchange for their commitment to complete the work selected for the sprint, the team receives a commitment from the organization that it will not change the contents of sprint for the duration of the sprint. If something so significant happens that the organization feels it needs to change the sprint, then the current sprint is aborted and a new sprint is started by beginning with another sprint planning meeting.

As the team selects items from the product backlog, they expand them into the more task-based sprint backlog. Each item on the product backlog may expand into one or more items on the sprint backlog, allowing the team to more effectively share the work.

The Sprint Review Meeting

Each sprint is required to deliver a *potentially shippable product increment*. This means that at the end of each month-long sprint the team has produced a coded, tested and usable piece of software. The software must be potentially shippable, meaning that the organization could choose to ship the software to customers (or use it internally) if enough new functionality is included to justify the overhead of shipping or deploying the new version. A commercial software distributor, for example, would probably not choose to ship a new version every month because of the upgrade hassles that could cause their customers. However, with Scrum the developers are required to produce a potentially shippable version each month.

At the end of each sprint, a sprint review meeting is held. During this meeting the team shows what they accomplished during the sprint. Typically this takes the form of a demo of the new features.

The sprint review meeting is intentionally kept very informal, typically with rules forbidding the use of PowerPoint slides and allowing no more than two hours of preparation time for the meeting. A sprint review meeting should not become a distraction or significant detour for the team; rather, it should be a natural result of the sprint.

The entire team as well as the product owner and ScrumMaster participate in the sprint review meeting. Others who are interested in the project (such as management, customers or engineers from other projects) may attend the sprint review if they desire.

During the sprint review meeting the project is assessed against the sprint goal that was previously determined during the sprint planning meeting. Ideally,

the team has completed each item planned for the sprint but it is more important that they achieve the overall goal of the sprint.

The Daily Scrum Meeting

Scrum is probably the first documented process to include a short daily meeting
(Beedle 1999), which in Scrum is called "the daily scrum." The idea, however,
has quickly spread to many of the other agile processes such as XP and Feature-
Driven Development. Whenever possible we want to choose the least time-consuming and the least-intrusive method of gathering and sharing project information. For many purposes, the daily scrum achieves exactly that goal.

The daily scrum is typically held as early as possible each day but after the
entire team has arrived for work. This is typically 9:00 or 9:30. Everyone on the
team is required to attend, including programmers, testers, the product owner
and the ScrumMaster. The meeting is kept short: usually 15 minutes or less and
never longer than 30. To keep the meeting short, some teams require participants to stand.

During the daily scrum each team member answers the following three questions:

1. What did you do yesterday?

2. What will you do today?

3. What obstacles are in in your way?

It is important that the daily scrum does not come across as a grilling by the
ScrumMaster. One of the goals of the meeting is to have each developer make
commitments in front of his or her peers. Commitments are not made to the
manager or the company but to each other.

The daily scrum should stick as closely as possible to the three questions
above, and should not move off into designing parts of the system or resolving
issues that were raised. Such items are noted during the meeting but are
resolved afterwards. It's OK to identify a subset of the team that will meet to
resolve an issue, but do not resolve issues during the daily scrum. For example,
suppose someone asks whether we should start using the recently released version 5.0 of our vendor's application server. In that case, we agree that right after
the daily scrum another meeting will occur between:

- the technical architect, who can assess the technical impact on using the
  new application server

- the product owner, who comes from the Marketing department and will be in the best position to decide if our customers will deploy the old or new application server

- a representative from the test team who can assess the impact on her group

The ScrumMaster is on hand as a facilitator and to make sure the meeting stays focused on the three questions and moves along at a brisk pace. The product owner is present because she will ideally have work to report on just like anyone else ("I finished writing tests for the 'Add book to shopping cart' story and today I'm going to do some market research on which cards we should accept. I should be able to finish that by the end of the day.").

One benefit to holding daily meetings is that they can serve as random checkpoints for senior managers or anyone else interested in the state of the project. By consistently meeting at the same time of day and extending a general "join us whenever you're interested" invitation, the team may be able to get out of more onerous meetings such as monthly project reviews. However, if non-team members are invited to the daily scrums, be sure to establish a rule that only people directly on the project can ask questions during the meeting. So, the Big Boss can attend and listen to her heart's content. She cannot, however, redirect the meeting by asking questions.

The daily scrum provides everyone on the team a quick daily snapshot of where things stand on the project. This makes it the perfect time for the team to reconsider current assignments. For example, suppose Randy reports that the story he's working on is taking much longer than he expected and Andrew reports that he is significantly ahead of schedule. In this case it may be appropriate for Andrew to spend the day paired with Randy and working on Randy's tasks or for Andrew to outright take on responsibility for some of Randy's tasks.

The ScrumMaster must walk a fine line during the daily scrums. She needs to keep the pace brisk but cannot let the meetings feel as though they are for her benefit alone. One question that should never be asked is "How much time do you have left on the 'Order a book' story?" This information is extremely important but if it is asked for during the daily scrum then the daily scrum will become all about estimates and numbers. Separate from the daily scrum meeting, I have the team update their estimates on a communal whiteboard or in the software we're using if we're not collocated.

Adding Stories to Scrum

Having described the general Scrum approach we now turn our attention to how Scrum can be improved by combining it with the use of stories.

Stories and the Product Backlog

I have had great success expressing Scrum backlog items in the form of user stories (Cohn 2003). Rather than allowing product backlog items to describe new features, issues to investigate, defects to be fixed, and so on, the product backlog is constrained to only user stories. Each story in the product backlog must describe some item of value to a user or to the product owner.

By constraining the product backlog to only user stories it becomes much easier for the product owner to prioritize the backlog. With all backlog items in terms she can understand, it becomes easy for the product owner to make decisions to trade one feature for another.

As with XP, in Scrum it is not important for the product owner to identify all of the requirements up front. However, there is often a benefit to jotting down as many of them as possible at the outset. Scrum has no prescribed, or even recommended, approach to initially stocking the product backlog. Traditionally this has happened through an unstructured discussion between the product owner, ScrumMaster, and one or more developers. However, I've found that by first identifying user roles and then focusing on the stories for each user role, Scrum is combined with a powerful requirements identification technique.

Stories in the Sprint Planning Meeting

During the sprint planning meeting, the product owner and team discuss the top priority items on the product backlog. The team then identifies the items they will commit to completing during the sprint. They then break those tasks into smaller tasks as necessary so that developers can sign up for tasks as the sprint progresses.

Stories force each product backlog item to each deliver value that the customer can assess. Because of this I have found that sprint planning meetings are easier to conduct and go faster than when the team is forced to explain the benefit of technology-driven backlog items such as "refactor the Login class to throw an exception."

Stories also fit well into sprint planning because, as we saw in Chapter 10, "Planning an Iteration," stories may be readily disaggregated into their constituent tasks.

Stories in the Sprint Review Meeting

The use of stories benefits Scrum during the sprint review meeting because stories make it simpler to assess what parts of a sprint have been completed. On a Scrum project that uses a random collection of technical tasks, requirements, issues and bug fixes as its product backlog, it can be difficult for the team to demonstrate that each item made its way into the product built during that sprint. When the entire product backlog is composed of stories describing items of customer or user value, it is generally easier to demonstrate those items.

Stories and the Daily Scrum Meeting

I have found stories beneficial to daily scrum meetings because they help ensure focus remains on customer and end-user desires. Because there is no upfront requirements or analyis phase that precedes a sprint, sprints are started with only a partial understanding of exactly what will be built. The team may know they are planning to add a search screen but they may not know what fields will be searchable, how search criteria may be combined, and so on. Stories are useful because they remind the team about the intent behind what is being developed. In the midst of a sprint the team can use the story (as well as ongoing discussions with the product owner about the story) to determine whether they have gone far enough, or perhaps too far, in programming a particular story.

A Case Study

As an example of adding stories to Scrum, let's consider a project I was involved in. The company, let's call them Cosmodemonic Biotech for convenience, was a small but publicly-traded developer of software for the life sciences industry. Cosmodemonic Biotech had just completed a nine-month development effort to introduce a new product for human geneticists. Shortly after the new product was delivered to its initial beta site, the company announced that it was being acquired.

The acquiring company was interested in the list of customers that came along with the product. However, they decided that the software would need to be rewritten for a variety of reasons, including:

- the client technologies of the original product (HTML) did not fit well with the strategic vision of the new owner

- the target market for the product changed from very large pharmaceutical companies with multi-terabyte databases to academic research labs and small biotech companies with much smaller databases

- a relatively poor implementation throughout much of the original code

The original product had been developed in a very strict waterfall manner over a period of nine months with a team that was as large as 100 developers. The new product would need to deliver essentially the same functionality but would have a team size of no more than seven.

To achieve this, we used Scrum augmented with user stories as described in this chapter. By all measures the project was a success. It took the Scrum team twelve months to complete what the waterfall team had done in nine. However, because the Scrum team never exceeded seven people, including the product owner and ScrumMaster, the project took 54 person-months to complete. The waterfall version had taken 540 person-months to complete.

The waterfall team produced 58,000 non-comment Java source statements. The Scrum with stories team did more with less, and produced 51,000. This means the waterfall team produced 120 Java source statements per person-month while the Scrum team produced 840 per person-month. These comparisons are shown in Table 15.2.

Table 15.2 *Comparison of the two approaches to the same project.*

	Waterfall	Scrum with Stories
Use Case Pages	3,000	0
Stories	0	1,400
Calendar Months	9	12
Person Months	540	54
Lines of Java Code	58,000	51,000
Lines of Java Code / Person-Month	120	840

Summary

- Scrum is an iterative and an incremental process.

- Scrum projects progress in a series of thirty-day iterations called sprints.

- A ScrumMaster fills the project manager role but is more leader and facilitator than manager.

- A typical Scrum team includes four to seven developers.

- The product backlog is a list of all desired features that have not yet been either added to the product or planned for the current sprint.

- The sprint backlog is a list of tasks the team has committed to for the current sprint.

- XP's customer role is played by the Scrum product owner.

- The product owner prioritizes the product backlog.

- At the start of the sprint, the team selects what and how much work they commit to completing during the sprint.

- Brief daily scrum meetings are held. During these meetings each team member says what she completed yesterday, what she'll complete today, and identifies any obstacles in her way.

- Each sprint is responsible for producing a potentially shippable product increment.

- At the end of sprint, the team demonstrates the software it created in a sprint review meeting.

Questions

15.1   Describe the differences between an incremental and an iterative process.

15.2   What is the relationship between the product backlog and the sprint backlog?

15.3   What is meant by a potentially shippable product increment?

15.4   Who is responsible for prioritizing work and for selecting the work the team will perform during a sprint?

15.5   What questions are answered by each team member at the daily scrum?

Chapter 16

Additional Topics

Throughout this part of the book we have looked at some topics that are frequently raised whenever user stories are discussed. We've looked at how user stories differ from other requirements methods and why user stories are preferable in some cases. We've looked at some common smells, or problems, with user stories and how to correct them. In this chapter we turn our attention to several additional topics:

- handling nonfunctional requirements

- whether teams should use paper note cards or software

- the impact of user stories on the user interface

- whether user stories should be retained after they have been developed

- the relationship between bug reports and stories

Handling NonFunctional Requirements

A common stumbling block for teams getting started with user stories is their feeling that everything must be conveyed as a user story. Most projects will encounter at least a few requirements that cannot be adequately reflected as stories. Frequently these will be a system's nonfunctional requirements.

Nonfunctional requirements can address a variety of system needs. Some of the more common types of nonfunctional requirements are found in the following areas:

- performance

- accuracy

- portability

- reusability

- maintainability

- interoperabilty

- availability

- usability

- security

- capacity

Many nonfunctional requirements can be considered as constraints on the system's behavior. For example, it is not uncommon for a project to include a requirement such as "The system shall be written in Java." This is clearly a constraint on the design of the rest of the system. As discussed in Chapter 7, "Guidelines for Good Stories," constraints are best handled by writing the constraint on a card and annotating the card with "Constraint." In most cases, an automated test can be written (and run at least daily) to ensure compliance with a constraint. A few constraints cannot be realistically tested or are not worth testing. The constraint "The system shall be written in Java" comes to mind. There are certainly easy ways to ensure this constraint is satisfied.

Examples of some common constraints are shown in Table 16.1. Beyond writing constraints on a card, if there are additional nonfunctional requirements that a system must adhere to, then communicate them in whatever form is appropriate or traditional. If, for example, the project can benefit from a data dictionary showing the size and type of all variables in the system, then create a data dictionary.

Table 16.1 *Sample constraints written for a variety of common nonfunctional requirements.*

Area	Sample Constraint
Performance	80% of database searches will return results to the screen in less than two seconds.
Accuracy	The software will correctly predict the winner of a football game at least 55% of the time.
Portability	The system shall not make use of any technology that would make it difficult to port to Linux.
Reusability	The database and database access code will be reusable in future applications.

Table 16.1 *Sample constraints written for a variety of common nonfunctional requirements. (Continued)*

Area	Sample Constraint
Maintainability	Automated unit tests must exist for all components. Automated unit tests must be run in their entirety at least once every 24 hours.
Interoperability	The system shall be written in Java. All configuration data shall be stored in XML files. Data shall be stored in MySQL.
Capacity	The database will be capable of storing 20 million members on the specified hardware while still meeting performance objectives.

Paper or Software?

Even more common than being asked "paper or plastic?" at the grocery store is the question of whether stories should be written on paper note cards or stored in a software system. Many in the Extreme Programming community advocate the use of paper note cards because of their simplicity. Extreme Programming places a premium on simple solutions, and paper note cards are definitely simple. Additionally, cards encourage interaction and discussion. They can be placed on a table in various formations during planning, they can be stacked and sorted, they can be carried into any meeting, and so on.

On the other hand, there are software products designed specifically for tracking stories (VersionOne,[1] XPlanner,[2] Select Scope Manager[3]) as well as general purpose software that can be used with stories (spreadsheets, defect trackers and wikis).

One of the main advantages that cards have over software is that their low-tech nature is a constant reminder that stories are imprecise. When shown in software, stories may take on the appearance of IEEE 830-style requirements and those writing stories may add additional, unnecessary detail because of that.

The typical note card can hold a limited amount of writing. This gives it a natural upper limit on the amount of text. This limitation does not exist in most software alternatives. On the other hand, a common practice among those

---

1. See www.versionone.net.
2. See www.xplanner.org
3. See www.selectbs.com/products/products/select_scope_manager.htm.

using note cards is to write some sample acceptance tests for a story on the back of the card. In many cases, the size of the card can work against it when writing the test cases.

Choosing Software at ClickTactics

ClickTactics is a marketing solutions provider that writes web-accessible software components. They started with note cards but switched to software, V1:XP from VersionOne.

Mark Mosholder, Senior Product Manager at ClickTactics, says one reason for the change is that their sales force and upper management are distributed across multiple sites. With remote stakeholders they could not say "go look at the board" so they spent a lot of time updating senior management and other remote stakeholders. Also, when using note cards they had problems with cards occasionally getting lost and then found weeks later in a pile under a desk.

Keeping stories in the VersionOne software allowed ClickTactics to promote their use of XP as a sales tool. Using the software, they give some customers limited visibility into their iterations. They then promote the speed with which they can turn around new versions for customers by telling them, "We can get you new functionality in three weeks."

Mark says there have been no drawbacks to their decision and says he would make the same decision again.

A project pursuing ISO (International Organization for Standardization), or similar, certification that requires traceability from a requirement statement down through code and tests will probably favor software. It should be possible to achieve ISO certification with handwritten note cards, but putting in place and demonstrating adequate change control procedures over a deck of cards probably outweighs the other advantages cards may have.

Similarly, a team that is not collocated will probably prefer software over note cards. When one or more developers, or especially the customer, is remote, it is too hard to work with paper.

An additional advantage to note cards is that they are very easy to sort and can be sorted in a variety of ways. A collection of stories can be sorted into high, medium and low priority piles. Or it could be sorted into more precise order with the first story higher priority than the second and the second higher priority than the third and so on.

Unlike many of the most devout supporters of either technique, my opinion is that both approaches can be appropriate. I recommend starting with cards and seeing how they work in your environment. Then, if there's a compelling reason to use software, switch.

Using a Wiki at Diaspar Software Services

J. B. Rainsberger is the founder of Diaspar Software Services, a software development and consulting company. As a consultant, J. B. cannot always be on-site with his customers. In those situations, J. B. uses a wiki to improve communication between himself and his remote customer. A wiki is a set of special web pages that can be edited by anyone viewing the page. J. B. and Diaspar Software use FitNesse as their wiki. Rather than writing a story card for each story they create a new page for each story.

J. B. reports that this worked extremely well on a recent small project. As he had questions about a story he would note the question on the page and add the text "todo." Several times a week his customer would check the wiki, search for "todo," and answer the questions. Urgent issues were handled by phone; but because of the efficiencies of using a wiki there were surprisingly few urgent issues. J. B. has worked with paper note cards on other projects but reports that on this project, with its remote customer, there was never a time when he wished he had the stories on cards as well as in the wiki.

Although J. B. uses the FitNesse wiki for writing executable tests for every project, he points out that "having everyone in the room makes it unnecessary to put stories on a wiki."

User Stories and the User Interface

It has been pointed out that agile methods largely ignore issues of designing the user interface. To some extent this is understandable: Agile processes are highly iterative, while traditional approaches to user interface design have been big-bang with heavy reliance on upfront design. It is important to understand the potential risks in pursuing an agile story-based approach for an application with a significant or important user interface.

It is one of the tenets of agile development that we may iteratively refine a system. User stories allow us to defer conversations until shortly before the developers are ready to add support for the story to the program. Sometimes deferring these conversations causes the developers to slightly rework existing parts of an application; but the belief is that the cost of these slight reworkings is more than justified by the savings in not holding requirements discussions about features that will later be dropped, and by the benefits of allowing the customer to steer the product with many smaller course corrections.

If these changes happen beneath the user interface of an application then this belief may be true. However, what happens when these changes affect the user interface? Larry Constantine (2002) writes that:

> For user interfaces, the architecture—the overall organization, the navigation, and the look–and–feel—must be designed to fit the full panoply of tasks to be covered. When it comes to the user interface, later refinement of the architecture is not as acceptable because it means changing the system for users who have already learned or mastered an earlier interface. Even small adjustments in the placement or form of features can be problematic for users.

This means that if the user interface will be important to the success of our product, then we might need to think about the user interface right from the start. If changing the user interface will cause problems for users then there is probably an unwritten constraint on the project—"Change the user interface as little as possible once it's started."

Constantine and Lockwood (2002) propose agile usage-centered design as a solution. Agile usage-centered design is driven by essential use cases or task cases rather than user stories. However, we can replace essential use cases with stories, which leads to the following story-based variation on Agile Usage-Centered Design:

1. Perform user role modeling.

2. Trawl for high-level user stories.

3. Prioritize stories.

4. Refine high- and medium-priority stories.

5. Organize stories into groups.

6. Create a paper prototype.

7. Refine the prototype.

8. Start programming.

The first step is to hold a user role modeling session, exactly as described in Chapter 3, "User Role Modeling." To complete the next few steps, initiate a story-writing workshop as described in Chapter 4, "Gathering Stories." In the workshop focus initially on capturing the highest-level stories, probably no more than two dozen.

Next, prioritize the high-level stories into three groups: High-priority stories must be in the upcoming release, medium-priority stories are desired for the upcoming release, and low priority stories can be deferred until a subsequent release. Put the low priority stories aside while refining the high- and medium-priority stories into smaller stories. These stories should be the size you will work with in planning the release.

Next, organize the high- and medium-priority stories into groups that have a high likelihood of being performed together. Then, draw prototypes on paper for each group of stories. After creating the paper prototypes, show them to users (or user proxies if necessary) and refine the prototypes based on their comments.

If you add these steps to your project, remember to keep the process as light-weight as you can. Some of the stories that were identified and that are being prototyped into a user interface could end up being removed from the project before they get developed. Avoid spending any more time than necessary. For most applications, this may entail somewhere from a few days to no more than a few weeks (for commercial software with remote users).

Write Two

A few years ago I was working on a project and we brought Ward Cunningham in to consult and assess the project. At the time the team was struggling with questions about the user interface. There were many hot-and-heavy debates about whether users would prefer a browser-based interface or whether they'd prefer a native application. Our marketing group had asked the users but we weren't confident that they had surveyed enough users or that they'd done the research the right way.

Ward settled the question by telling us "Write two user interfaces." His logic was that neither would be hard to write and between the two of them, they would keep the application's middle-tier honest. With two user interfaces no functionality would be inappropriately moved to the client tier if doing so meant that functionality would have to be written twice.

Ward's suggestion was right. We, of course, failed to listen, thinking it would be too expensive to develop two complete user interfaces. When the product was finished our customers let us know that we had indeed chosen the wrong user interface technology. And a project was quickly begun to add a second user interface.

Retaining the Stories

Arguments over whether stories should be retained are common. On one side are those who say that the pleasure of ripping up a completed card outweighs any value of retaining the card. On the opposite side is the more conservative crowd who would rather save the story than risk throwing it away and then needing it later.

If you're using software to hold your stories there is very little reason to get rid of completed stories. You may get some pleasure and feelings of closure from deleting an electronic story but it's probably not as great as the visceral pleasure of ripping a physical card in half.

If you're using paper note cards, then there can indeed be a tangible pleasure associated with finishing a card and ripping it in half. I've used cards to guide the writing of this book and each time I complete a new section or revision I rip up the card. However, when I'm working on a software project, rather than a book, I prefer to retain the cards, archiving them on a shelf with a rubber band.

Over the years I've been involved in a handful of situations where I've been thankful that I retained the requirements. Here are some of the cases:

- The company I was working for was being bought. The acquiring company was intrigued by our lightweight software development process but they had their own heavily waterfall-oriented approach with numerous gates and sign-off points each project had to pass through. Because I was able to actually show them our process (from stories to code and tests) they allowed us to continue with our process and not adopt the company-wide standard. Even better, we were eventually able to make some inroads in spreading our process into other divisions of the company.

- On a number of occasions I've been involved in completely rewriting commercial products. In one case the first version of a product was a commercial failure because of some poor technology choices. The product was completely rewritten and became a moderate success. Another product was a phenomenal success as a client-server application, and five years later the company wanted it rewritten and available on the web. Whenever there were even outdated stories or requirements, they were useful to have around.

- In yet another situation I was involved with a small startup that was trying to close a deal with a much larger company. If the deal was closed it would push the company into profitable territory, and the boss was also promising high five-digit bonuses to all of the developers. We were asked to "provide a copy of the requirements." I started to go down the road of describing how we didn't really focus on written requirements and that we instead focused on conversation and collaboration. I could sense the conversation was not going to end well and that company profitability and the large developer bonuses were evaporating. I shifted gears and told them how we wrote requirements in the form of user stories. They liked the idea. Fortunately our stories were stored electronically on that project. We cut them from the system they were in, pasted them into a Word document, added a cover page and a signature page and everyone was happy.

Considering the variety of occasions on which I've found it useful to have retained stories, my recommendation is that you do so as well. If you're using software, either keep the software installed or print a report from it and file the report somewhere. If you're using cards, either save the cards themselves or photocopy them three at a time onto paper.

Stories for Bugs

A very common question is the relationship between stories and bug reports. What I've found to work best is to consider each bug report its own story. If fixing a bug is likely to take as long as a typical story, that bug can be treated just like any other story. However, for bugs that the team expects to be able to fix quickly, you should combine the bugs into one or more stories. With cards you can easily do this by stapling the story cards together along with a cover story card. Then, for planning purposes, the collection of bugs may be treated as a single story.

What About Colors?

Some teams favor using cards of different colors to indicate the type of story on the card. For example, traditional white cards could be used for normal stories. Red cards could be used for bugs, blue cards could be used for engineering tasks and so on.

To me, using colored cards always seems like a good idea in theory; but in practice is not worth the extra hassle. Instead of just keeping a supply of white cards in my pocket, I have to make sure to always carry a few of each color. If I run out and write the story on whatever is available I then need to rewrite the story later. But if you think colors will help you organize your stories, try it. I'll stick to what's simple—a huge pile of white cards.

Summary

- Nonfunctional requirements (such as for performance, accuracy, portability, reusability, maintainability, interoperability, capacity and so on) can often be handled by creating constraint cards. If the system has requirements that are more complex than this, supplement your user story approach with whatever additional format or technique best expresses those requirements.

- Neither note cards nor a software system is the best way to write stories in all cases. Match the tool to the project and team.

- An iterative process can lead to iterative changes in the user interface. Users, who become accustomed to very specific aspects of the interface, do not like user interface changes that affect how they have learned to operate the software. Consider adding some practices from Agile Usage-Centered Design to avoid iterating the user interface.

- There's a certain joy in ripping up a story card as soon as it's complete. But there are also reasons to retain the cards. Err on the safe side and retain the stories.

- Staple small bug reports together with a cover story card and treat them as a single story.

Developer Responsibilities

- You are responsible for suggesting and using alternative techniques and methods for expressing requirements when appropriate.

- You share a responsibility to decide what is right for your project: note cards or a software system.

- You share a responsibility for understanding the advantages and disadvantages of considering the overall user interface at the start of the project.

Customer Responsibilities

- You are responsible for requesting or using alternative techniques and methods for expressing requirements if you do not feel user stories are accurately reflecting some part of the requirements.

- You share a responsibility to decide what is right for your project: note cards or a software system.

- You share a responsibility for understanding the advantages and disadvantages of considering the overall user interface at the start of the project.

Questions

16.1   How should you handle a requirement for a system to scale up to use by 1,000 concurrent users?

16.2   Do you prefer to write stories on note cards or in a software system? Defend your answer.

16.3   What impact does an iterative process have on the user interface of an application?

16.4   Give some examples of systems that could benefit from more upfront consideration of the user interface than is typically given on an agile project.

16.5   Do you recommend retaining or disposing of stories once the story has been developed? Defend your answer.

PART IV

An Example

Part IV brings everything together in a comprehensive example. In the chapters that follow, you'll meet South Coast Nautical Supplies and some of its employees as they create a website to augment their print catalog. You'll have the opportunity to identify user roles, write stories with Lori (South Coast's vice president of Sales and Marketing and the customer for this project), estimate the stories, create a release plan and then write some acceptance tests for the stories in the initial plan.

Chapter 17

The User Roles

Over the course of the next five chapters we will undertake a small, hypothetical project. In this chapter we'll start by identifying the key user roles. In subsequent chapters we'll move on to writing stories, estimating the stories, planning a release, and writing acceptance tests for the stories in the release.

The Project

Our company, South Coast Nautical Supplies, has been selling sailing supplies through a print catalog for thirty years. Our catalogs feature items such as Global Positioning Systems, clocks, weather equipment, navigation and plotting equipment, life rafts, inflatable vests, charts, maps and books. So far our Internet presence has been a simple one-page site directing people to call a toll-free number to request a catalog.

Our boss has decided we should finally get with the times and start selling things over the Internet. However, rather than start by selling some of our bigger ticket items, he wants us to start by selling just books. Some items in our catalog cost over $10,000 and until we know our site works well and doesn't lose orders, we don't want to take any risk with expensive items. But if we find that our customers like being able to order online, and if we do a good job on the site, we'll expand and sell the rest of our products on the site.

Oh, and the last thing the boss says is that the site needs to be live in thirty days so we can capture increased sales during the peak summer sailing months.

Identifying the Customer

The project needs a customer to help us identify and write stories. The customers for this product are the sailors who buy the books and they are all outside

191

the company. So, we need an internal customer who can act as a proxy for the real end-user customers. For this the boss designates Lori, who is the vice president of Sales and Marketing.

In an initial meeting with Lori she provides more background on the system she needs. She wants a "typical bookstore/eCommerce site." She wants customers to be able to search for books in a variety of ways (we don't push for clarification at this point), she wants users to be able to maintain lists of books they'll buy later, she wants users to rate and review books they buy, and she wants to them users check on the status of an order. We've seen plenty of sites like this so we tell Lori we're ready to start.

Identifying Some Initial Roles

The first thing we do is gather some of the developers together with Lori in a room with a large table. Lori has already researched the market and knows the demographics of our typical customers. Lori and the developers write the following user role cards, which are placed as shown in Figure 17.1:

- Hardcore Sailor
- Novice Sailor
- New Sailor
- Gift-Buyer
- Non-Sailing Spouse
- Administrator
- Sales Vice President
- Charter Captain
- Experienced Sailor
- Sailing School
- Library
- Instructor

Consolidating and Narrowing

After the user role names are written on cards we need to remove duplicates or near duplicates, consider whether any roles should be merged, and come up with a refined list of user roles that the project will start with. The easiest way to start is by trying to remove any card that is placed entirely on top of another card, indicating that its author thought they were duplicates.

In this case, the New Sailor card has been placed on top of the Novice Sailor card. The authors of those cards explain what they intended by them, and anyone else adds any remarks they wish. It turns out that there is a distinction between a Novice Sailor and a New Sailor. A New Sailor is someone who is new to the sport of sailing; perhaps she is currently taking lessons or has sailed a few times. The author of the Novice Sailor card actually meant that role to represent someone who may have been sailing for years but just not often enough to have become good at it. The group decides that although these roles appear to be slightly different, they are not sufficiently different that it is worth having two roles for them. They are merged together in a single role, Novice Sailor, and the New Sailor card is torn up and thrown away.

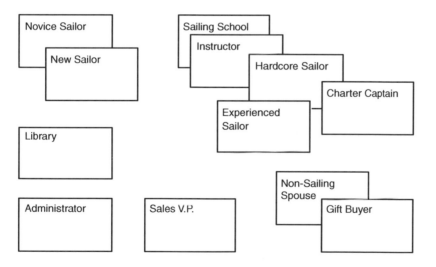

Figure 17.1 *Positioning the user role cards.*

Next, the group considers the overlapping Sailing School and Instructor cards. The author of the Instructor card explains that the role represents sailors who teach sailing classes. Instructors, she argues, frequently buy copies of books for their students or perhaps assemble lists of books that students are required to read. The author of the Sailing School role card indicates that this is partially what she intended for that card. However, she thought that typical use would be by an administrator at the school rather than by the sailing instructor himself. Lori the customer clears this up for us by telling us that even if it is a school administrator, the administrator will have many of the same characteristics of an Instructor. Since an Instructor is more clearly a single person than is Sailing School, the Sailing School card is torn up.

The Hardcore Sailor card has been postioned so that it partially overlaps Instructor, Experienced Sailor and even the Charter Captain role cards. The group discusses these roles next and learns that the Hardcore Sailor role was written to capture the type of sailor who typically knows exactly which books she wants. The Hardcore Sailor knows, for example, the name of the best book on navigation. Her search patterns will therefore be quite different from those of a less knowledgeable sailor, even an Experienced Sailor. The Experienced Sailor role represents people very familiar with the products the site will offer but who may not automatically recall the names of the best books.

After discussing Charter Captain, the team decides that role is essentially the same as Hardcore Sailor and the card is torn up.

At this point, the team has decided to keep Novice Sailor, Instructor, Hardcore Sailor, and Experienced Sailor. They've disposed of New Sailor, Charter Captain, and Sailing School. And they have yet to consider Gift-Buyer, Non-Sailing Spouse, Administrator, and Sales Vice President. The authors of these remaining role cards explain their intent.

The Gift Buyer role represents someone who is not a sailor but who is buying a gift for someone who is. The author of the Non-Sailing Spouse role indicates that this was the intent behind that card. After some discussion about the two role cards the team decides to tear both up and replace them with a consolidated card for the Non-Sailing Gift Buyer role.

The author of the Administrator role explains that this role represents the work that will be done by one or more administrators who will need to load data into the system and otherwise keep the system running. This is the first role the team talks about that represents someone who is not buying items from the site. After discussing it, they decide that the role is important, and Lori indicates that she will have some stories about how the system will be maintained and how new items will be added to the site's inventory.

The Sales Vice President role is discussed next. This is another non-purchasing role. However, the CEO has mandated that the new system be watched very closely to see how it is affecting sales. The team considers leaving the role out because they don't think there will be many stories specifically for the role. In the end they decide to include the role but to rename it to the more generic Report Viewer.

The Library role is discussed. For a moment the team thinks it might be similar to either a Sailing School or even a Non-Sailing Spouse. However, the group rejects these ideas and decides to keep Library as a role. However, in keeping with the guideline to create roles that represent discrete users, the Library card is ripped up and replaced with a Librarian card.

At this point the team has settled on the roles shown in Figure 17.2.

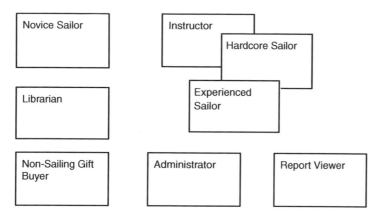

Figure 17.2 *The roles after consolidation and initial discussion.*

Role Modeling

Next, the team considers each role and adds detail to the role cards. The details will vary based on the domain and the type of software but good, general factors to consider include:

- The frequency with which the user will use the software.

- The user's level of expertise with the domain.

- The user's general level of proficiency with computers and software.

- The user's level of proficiency with the software being developed.

- The user's general goal for using the software. Some users are after convenience, others favor a rich experience, and so on.

The group discusses these issues for each role card. They update the user role cards as follows:

Novice Sailor: Experienced web shopper. Expected to make 6 purchases during first 3 months of sailing. Is sometimes referred to a specific title; other times needs help selecting the right book. Wants more help in selecting appropriate books (good content written at the appropriate level) than she gets in a physical bookstore.

Instructor: Expected to use the website frequently, often once a week. Through the company's telephone sales group, an Instructor frequently places similar orders (for example, 20 copies of the same book). Proficient with the website but usually somewhat nervous around computers. Interested in getting the best prices. Not interested in reviews or other "frills."

Hard Core Sailor: Generally inexperienced with computers. A large purchaser of items from the company's catalog but not a large purchaser of books. Buys lots of additional equipment from us. Usually knows exactly what he's looking for. Doesn't want to feel stupid while trying to use the site.

Experienced Sailor: Proficient with computers. Expected to order once or twice per quarter, perhaps more often during the summer. Knowledgeable about sailing but usually only for local regions. Very interested in what other sailors say are the best products and the best places to sail.

Non-Sailing Gift Buyer: Usually proficient with computers (or would not chose to purchase a gift online). Not a sailor and will have passing familiarity at best with sailing terms. Will usually be after a very specific book but may be looking for a book on a given topic.

Librarian: Proficient with computers. Knows exactly what she is looking for and prefers to order by ISBN rather than author or even title. Not particularly interested in frills such as gift wrapping or tracking shipments. Will generally place a small number of orders per year but each order will be for more books than a typical individual order.

Administrator: Highly proficient with computers. Has at least a passing familiarity with sailing. Accesses the back-end of the system daily as part of her job. Interested in quickly learning the software but will want advanced user shortcuts later.

Report Viewer: Moderate proficiency with computers, mostly with business programs such as spreadsheets and word processors. Interested in highly detailed data on how the system is working, what visitors are buying or not buying, and how they are navigating or searching the site. Very willing to trade speed for power and depth.

Adding Personas

It is sometimes worth spending a few minutes adding a persona to the work done thus far. The team asks Lori which of these user roles must absolutely be satisfied with the new website in order for it to succeed. She says that Hardcore Sailors are important because of their longevity as customers. But, even though they sail frequently, they are not large purchasers of books. On the other hand, the large population of Experienced Sailors is important and that group buys a significant number of books. Lori adds that perhaps the most important role to satisfy is the Instructor. Instructors can be responsible for the sale of hundreds of books throughout the year. In fact, she continues, with the new website she'd like to investigate ways of eventually offering financial incentives to Instructors who refer their students to the site.

With this information in mind the team decides to develop two personas. The first persona is Teresa. Teresa has been sailing for four years. She is the CEO of a publicly-traded biotech company and is completely comfortable ordering online. Teresa sails mainly during the summer so she'll only use the site during spring or summer, when preparing for a cruise. She's very busy and is interested in using our site to save time and to find books she hasn't seen before. Teresa is married to Tom, who doesn't sail himself but has accompanied Teresa on on two cruises through the Mediterranean.

The second persona is Captain Ron. Captain Ron has been sailing for 40 years and runs a sailing school out of San Diego. He retired from teaching high school five years ago and has been a sailing instructor ever since. He's been a loyal catalog customer for ten years. He's still a little intimidated by the computer in his office but he's intrigued enough by ordering on the web that we expect him to give it a try.

A Caveat about Teresa and Captain Ron

It's debatable whether it is worth adding personas to this system. Only add a persona if doing so helps your team think through stories for a critical-to-satisfy user of your system. For the South Coast Nautical Supplies system described in these chapters, it's probably not worth the extra effort.

However, since personas can be a valuable addition to your toolbox, I have included Teresa and Captain Ron in order to provide a more complete example.

Chapter 18

The Stories

To generate the initial list of stories, the team decides to convene a story writing workshop where they will dedicate an hour or two to writing as many stories as they can. During a story writing workshop, one approach is to just write stories in any order regardless of which role or persona may act in the story. An alternative approach is to start with a specific user role or persona and write all the stories the team can think of before moving onto the next role or persona. The results should be the same with either approach. In this case the team discusses it and chooses to work through each role and persona.

Stories for Teresa

The team decides to start with Teresa, a persona identified in the previous chapter, since the team's customer member, Lori, has said that it is critical that the new website satisfy Teresa. The team knows Teresa is looking for speed and convenience. She's a true power user and will not mind a little extra complexity as long as the complexity helps her find what she's looking for more quickly. The first story they write is Story Card 18.1.

A user can search for books by author, title or ISBN number.

▦ Story Card 18.1

The developers have some questions about this story. For example, can the user search by author, title and ISBN at the same time, or does Lori want them to search by only one criterion at a time? They let these questions sit for now and focus on getting more preliminary stories written down.

Next, Lori says that after searching for a book a user can see detailed information about a book. She gives a few examples of the type of information she means and then writes Story Card 18.2.

A user can view detailed information on a book. For example, number of pages, publication date and a brief description.

■ Story Card 18.2

There's probably more she'll want besides these three details but the developers can ask her later when they're ready to code this story.

As a typical eCommerce site, the team knows that users will need a "shopping cart" and that users will buy the books in their shopping carts. Lori the customer also says that a user will need the chance to delete books from the shopping cart before the order is processed. This leads to Story Card 18.3 and Story Card 18.4.

A user can put books into a "shopping cart" and buy them when she is done shopping.

■ Story Card 18.3

A user can remove books from her cart before completing an order.

■ Story Card 18.4

To actually process an order with a credit card, the system will need to know the credit card to charge and some address information. This leads to Story Card 18.5.

To buy a book the user enters her billing address, the shipping address and credit card information.

■ Story Card 18.5

Lori reminds the developers that since Teresa has only been sailing for four years, she won't always know exactly what book she wants. For Teresa the site should include features for customers to rate and review items. This leads Lori to write Story Card 18.6.

> A user can rate and review books.

■ Story Card 18.6

Since Teresa wants to be able to order as quickly as possible, the team decides that the system needs to remember shipping and billing information. Some of the site's customers, for example the Non-Sailing Gift Buyer role, may not buy very often so these customers may not want to create a reusable account. Similarly, any extra steps the first time may scare off Captain Ron who is always a little tentative with new websites. So, Lori decides that a user can buy books with or without an account and writes Story Card 18.7 and Story Card 18.8.

> A user can establish an account that remembers shipping and billing information.

■ Story Card 18.7

> A user can edit her account information (credit card, shipping address, billing address and so on).

■ Story Card 18.8

The team also knows that Teresa wants to put items on a wish list of items she wants but is not ready to buy today. She'll either buy them for herself later or she'll tell her husband, Tom, and he'll buy items from her wish list. So, Lori writes Story Card 18.9 and Story Card 18.10.

We want to make sure that whoever programs Story Card 18.10 knows that a user can select items from her own or someone else's wish list. We make sure to note that on the card (parenthetically in this case).

> A user can put books into a "wish list" that is visible to other site visitors.

■ Story Card 18.9

> A user can place an item from a wish list (even someone else's) into his or her shopping cart.

■ Story Card 18.10

Because speed will be important to Teresa, Lori also identifies a performance constraint relating to how long it takes to order a book. She writes Story Card 18.11.

> A repeat customer must be able to find one book and complete an order in less than 90 seconds.
> (Constraint)

■ Story Card 18.11

In this case Lori has chosen to focus on the time it takes a repeat customer to search for a book and complete her order. This is a good performance requirement because it captures all aspects of the user's experience with the site. Blazing fast database queries and middleware don't count for much if the user interface is so confusing to navigate that it takes a user three minutes to get to the search screen. This story reflects this better than would a story like "Searches must complete in two seconds." Naturally, Lori can add more performance constraints but it is usually sufficient to pick a few broad ones like this story.

Stories for Captain Ron

It becomes clear that the team is running out of stories for Teresa, the Experienced Sailor. So, they agree to switch focus to Captain Ron, who runs a sailing school and is a little more tentative with computers than is Teresa. When Captain Ron comes to the site he typically knows exactly what he's looking for. This leads Lori to write Story Card 18.12 and Story Card 18.13.

> A user can view a history of all of his past orders.

■ Story Card 18.12

> A user can easily re-purchase items when viewing past orders.

■ Story Card 18.13

These stories will allow Captain Ron to look back at his old orders and repurchase items from those orders. However, Lori points out that Captain Ron may also want to purchase an item that he looked at recently, even if he hasn't previously purchased it. She writes Story Card 18.14.

> The site always tells a shopper what the last 3 (?) items she viewed are and provides links back to them. (This works even between sessions.)

■ Story Card 18.14

Stories for a Novice Sailor

Next, the team moves on to consider the Novice Sailor role. The needs of a Novice Sailor largely overlap those of Teresa and Captain Ron. But Lori decides it would be helpful if a Novice Sailor could see a list of our recommendations. Here the Novice Sailor could find the books we recommend on a variety of topics. She writes Story Card 18.15.

> A user can see what books we recommend on a variety of topics.

■ Story Card 18.15

Stories for a Non-Sailing Gift Buyer

Switching to the Non-Sailing Gift Buyer role, the team discusses how it must be easy for a shopper to find the wish list of another person. They start to discuss various design solutions and what fields will be used for searching until they remember that design discussions should be saved for later. Instead of designing the feature in this meeting, Lori writes Story Card 18.16.

> A user, especially a Non-Sailing Gift Buyer, can easily find the wish lists of other users.

■ Story Card 18.16

Lori also knows that the system needs to support gift cards and wrapping. She writes Story Card 18.17 and Story Card 18.18.

> A user can choose to have items gift wrapped.

■ Story Card 18.17

> A user can choose to enclose a gift card and can write her own message for the card.

■ Story Card 18.18

Stories for a Report Viewer

Lori says that the system needs to generate reports on purchase and traffic patterns and so on. She hasn't yet thought about the reports in detail so the developers write a simple placeholding story that will remind them that there are reports to develop. They'll decide on the report contents later. For now she writes Story Card 18.19.

Thinking about reports reminds Lori that the reports are highly sensitive. Naturally, they won't be available from the main site that consumers see. But, she says that only certain people within the company can have access to the

> A Report Viewer can see reports of daily purchases broken down by book category, traffic, best- and worst-selling books and so on.

■ Story Card 18.19

reports. This could mean that if you can access one report you can access them all, or it could mean some users can access only some reports. The developers don't ask Lori about that now and Lori writes Story Card 18.20.

> A user must be properly authenticated before viewing reports.

■ Story Card 18.20

To make reports meaningful, Lori says that the database used by the website must be the same database used by our current telephone-based system. This leads Lori to write the constraint shown on Story Card 18.21.

> Orders made on the website have to end up in the same order database as telephone orders.
> (Constraint)

■ Story Card 18.21

Some Administration Stories

At this point attention shifts to the Administrator user role. The team thinks instantly of Story Card 18.22 and Story Card 18.23.

> An administrator can add new books to the site.

■ Story Card 18.22

> An administrator needs to approve or reject reviews before they're available on the site.

■ Story Card 18.23

The story about adding new books reminds them that administrators need to delete books and also edit books in case incorrect information was used when the book was added. So they write Story Card 18.24 and Story Card 18.25.

> An administrator can delete a book.

■ Story Card 18.24

> An administrator can edit the information about an existing book.

■ Story Card 18.25

Wrapping Up

By now Lori is starting to run out of stories. So far, each story has come instantly to mind but now she's having to think about whether there are any others. Because the project will be done using an incremental and iterative development process, it's not important that she think of every story right up front. But because she wants a preliminary estimate of how long the system will take to build, the team does want to think of as much as they can without spending an inordinate amount of time. If Lori comes up with a new story once we've started, she'll have the opportunity to move it into the release if she moves out the same approximate amount of work.

The developers ask Lori if there are any other stories she feels have been forgotten thus far. She writes Story Card 18.26.

Lori also reminds the developers that scalability needs are not tremendous but that the site does need to handle at least 50 concurrent users. They write this constraint on Story Card 18.27.

A user can check the status of her recent orders. If an order hasn't shipped, she can add or remove books, change the shipping method, the delivery address and the credit card.

■ Story Card 18.26

The system must support peak usage of up to 50 concurrent users.
(Constraint)

■ Story Card 18.27

Chapter 19

Estimating the Stories

The story writing workshop resulted in 27 stories, which are summarized in Table 19.1. The next goal is to create a release plan that will show Lori the customer what the developers expect to accomplish and whether the site can be operational within the boss's thirty day deadline. Because there is probably more work than can be completed in those thirty days, the developers will need to work closely with Lori to prioritize stories.

Table 19.1 *The initial collection of stories.*

Story Text
A user can search for books by author, title or ISBN number.
A user can view detailed information on a book. For example, number of pages, publication date and a brief description.
A user can put books into a "shopping cart" and buy them when she is done shopping.
A user can remove books from her cart before completing an order.
To buy a book the user enters her billing address, the shipping address and credit card information.
A user can rate and review books.
A user can establish an account that remembers shipping and billing information.
A user can edit her account information (credit card, shipping address, billing address and so on).
A user can put books into a "wish list" that is visible to other site visitors.
A user can place an item from a wish list (even someone else's) into his or her shopping cart.
A repeat customer must be able to find one book and complete an order in less than 90 seconds.
A user can view a history of all of his past orders.
A user can easily re-purchase items when viewing past orders.

Table 19.1 *The initial collection of stories. (Continued)*

Story Text
The site always tells a shopper what the last 3 (?) items she viewed are and provides links back to them. (This works even between sessions.)
A user can see what books we recommend on a variety of topics.
A user, especially a Non-Sailing Gift Buyer, can easily find the wish lists of other users.
A user can choose to have items gift wrapped.
A user can choose to enclose a gift card and can write her own message for the card.
A Report Viewer can see reports of daily purchases broken down by book category, traffic, best- and worst-selling books and so on.
A user must be properly authenticated before viewing reports.
Orders made on the website have to end up in the same order database as telephone orders.
An administrator can add new books to the site.
An administrator needs to approve or reject reviews before they're available on the site.
An administrator can delete a book.
An administrator can edit the information about an existing book.
A user can check the status of her recent orders. If an order hasn't shipped, she can add or remove books, change the shipping method, the delivery address and the credit card.
The system must support peak usage of up to 50 concurrent users.

In order to create the release plan an estimate is needed for each story. As we learned in Chapter 8, "Estimating User Stories," the developers are going to estimate each story in story points that represent ideal time, complexity, or some other measure meaningful to the team.

The First Story

It isn't necessary to start with the first story in this list ("A user can search for books by author, title or ISBN number") but in this case the first story is a good one to start estimating with. When Lori wrote this story, the developers weren't sure if Lori meant that a user could search for all of these fields at the same time or whether a user could search only one at a time. Since Lori's answer could have a big impact on the estimate, it's worth asking her.

Naturally Lori says she wants both. She wants a basic search mode where the value in one field searches both author and title. She then wants an advanced search screen where any or all of these fields can be used in combination. Even with both search modes the story isn't that big; but there's such an easy division between the modes that everyone agrees to tear up the story and replace it with Story Card 19.1 and Story Card 19.2.

> A user can do a basic simple search that searches for a word or phrase in both the author and title fields.

■ Story Card 19.1

> A user can search for books by entering values in any combination of author, title and ISBN.

■ Story Card 19.2

To estimate the stories, three programmers—Rafe, Jay and Maria—get together in a room with Lori, the customer. They bring along the story cards and a few dozen blank cards. The programmers talk about Story Card 19.1, clarify a few details on it by asking questions of Lori, and then each programmer writes his or her estimate on an index card. When everyone is done, each programmer holds his or her card up so everyone can see it. They've written:

Rafe: 1
Jay: ½
Maria: 2

These three developers discuss their estimates. Maria explains why she thinks this story is worth two story points. She talks about how they'll need to select a search engine, incorporate it, and only then be able to write the screens to fulfill the story. Jay says that he's already familiar with all likely searching options and is pretty confident about the direction they should go, which is why his estimate is so much lower.

Everyone is asked to write down a new estimate. When they're down they again show their cards. This time the cards say:

Rafe: 1
Jay: 1
Maria: 1

That was pretty easy. Jay decided to move his estimate up and Maria was convinced that they could do the story faster than she originally thought. They now have a one-story point estimate to use for Story Card 19.1. They start writing estimates down as shown in Table 19.2.

Table 19.2 *Starting to write down the estimates.*

Story	Estimate
A user can do a basic simple search that searches for a word or phrase in both the author and title fields.	1

Note that Lori the customer is present while the programmers come up with these estimates but she isn't participating by writing down her estimates. Since Lori isn't a programmer on the project, she isn't allowed to estimate. Further, she's not allowed to gasp or otherwise express shock at an estimate. If she does, she'll undermine the estimation effort. Of course, if Lori hears an estimate that sounds way out of line (either too high or too low) she may need to provide some guidance or clarification. For example, she may offer something along the lines of "I can see how that might be ten story points as you're describing it but I think I'm asking for something much, much simpler. All I really want is …"

Advanced Search

On to Story Card 19.2, the advanced search. The programmers again write their estimates on index cards and turn them over at the same time showing:

Rafe: 2
Jay: 1
Maria: 2

Rafe says the advanced search will take a little longer than the basic search because there's more to search on. Jay agrees but says that since the basic search will have already been coded, it won't take long to add the advanced search features. However, Maria points out that the stories are independent and we don't know which story will be done first. Lori the customer says she's not sure which she'll want done first. She's inclined to have the basic search done first but won't be sure until she knows the estimate (that is, cost) of each.

After another round or two of writing estimates on cards, everyone agrees that while there is a bit more work on the advanced search than the basic search, it isn't much and they should again use an estimate of one story point.

The next few stories are straightforward to estimate and none need to be split. The developers arrive at the estimates shown in Table 19.3.

Table 19.3 *Building up the list of estimates.*

Story	Estimate
A user can do a basic simple search that searches for a word or phrase in both the author and title fields.	1
A user can search for books by entering values in any combination of author, title and ISBN.	1
A user can view detailed information on a book. For example, number of pages, publication date and a brief description.	1
A user can put books into a "shopping cart" and buy them when she is done shopping.	1
A user can remove books from her cart before completing an order.	½
To buy a book the user enters her billing address, the shipping address and credit card information.	2

Rating and Reviewing

The next story ("A user can rate and review books") is a bit harder. Before writing down estimates and showing them to each other, the developers talk about this story. The rating part doesn't seem hard but the reviews seem more complicated. They'll need a screen for users to enter a review and maybe to preview it. Will reviews just be plain text or can the reviewer type in HTML? Can users only review books they bought from us?

Because reviews are so much more involved than just rating books, we decide to split the story. This leads to Story Card 19.3 and Story Card 19.4.

A user can rate books from 1 (bad) to 5 (good). The book does not have to be one the user bought from us.

Story Card 19.3

The programmers estimate Story Card 19.3 as two points and Story Card 19.4 as four story points.

> A user can write a review of a book. She can preview the review
> before submitting it. The book does not have to be one the user
> bought from us.

■ Story Card 19.4

While they're thinking about rating and reviewing books, they also consider "An administrator needs to approve or reject reviews before they're available on the site." This could be really simple, or it could be more involved and require the administrator to identify the reason she rejects a review or possibly email the reviewer. The programmers don't think Lori will want anything complicated and their discussion leads to an estimate of two story points.

Accounts

The next story ("A user can establish an account that remembers shipping and billing information") seems straightforward and the developers estimate it at two story points.

Next, the developers start to estimate "A user can edit her account information (credit card, shipping address, billing address and so on)." This story is not very large but it is easily split. Splitting a story like this one is frequently a good idea because it allows more flexibility during release planning and it allows the customer to prioritize work at a much finer level. In our case, for example, Lori may think it is critical for users to edit their credit cards but she may be willing to wait a few iterations for the ability for users to change addresses. The original story is split, resulting in Story Card 19.5 and Story Card 19.6. Neither of

> A user can edit the credit card information stored in her
> account.

■ Story Card 19.5

> A user can edit the shipping and billing addresses stored in her
> account.

■ Story Card 19.6

these stories seems difficult so the programmers estimate Story Card 19.5 as ½ story point and Story Card 19.6 as one point.

Finishing the Estimates

This same process is repeated for each of the remaining stories. Only a few of the remaining stories are worth specific mention. First is the vague story: "A user, especially a Non-Sailing Gift Buyer, can easily find the wish lists of other users." When asked about her intentions regarding how users could search for a wish list, Lori provides enough detail that the story can be rewritten as Story Card 19.7.

> A user, especially a Non-Sailing Gift Buyer, can search for a wish list based on its owner's name and state.

■ Story Card 19.7

Next, everyone agrees to split "A user can check the status of her recent orders. If an order hasn't shipped, she can add or remove books, change the shipping method, the delivery address and the credit card." One story will cover checking the status of a recent order; the second story covers changing orders that haven't yet shipped. The stories are shown on Story Card 19.8 and Story Card 19.9.

> A user can check the status of her recent orders.

■ Story Card 19.8

> If an order hasn't shipped, a user can add or remove books, change the shipping method, the delivery address and the credit card.

■ Story Card 19.9

Finally, these three stories are constraints:

- A repeat customer must be able to find one book and complete an order in less than 90 seconds.

- Orders made on the website have to end up in the same order database as telephone orders.

- The system must support peak usage of up to 50 concurrent users.

As constraints they influence other stories but do not require any specific coding themselves.

All the Estimates

Table 19.4 shows all of the estimates.

Table 19.4 *The complete list of stories and estimates.*

Story	Estimate
A user can do a basic simple search that searches for a word or phrase in both the author and title fields.	1
A user can search for books by entering values in any combination of author, title and ISBN.	1
A user can view detailed information on a book. For example, number of pages, publication date and a brief description.	1
A user can put books into a "shopping cart" and buy them when she is done shopping.	1
A user can remove books from her cart before completing an order.	½
To buy a book the user enters her billing address, the shipping address and credit card information.	2
A user can rate books from 1 (bad) to 5 (good). The book does not have to be one the user bought from us.	2
A user can write a review of a book. She can preview the review before submitting it. The book does not have to be one the user bought from us.	4
An administrator needs to approve or reject reviews before they're available on the site.	2
A user can establish an account that remembers shipping and billing information.	2
A user can edit the credit card information stored in her account.	½
A user can edit the shipping and billing addresses stored in her account.	1

Table 19.4 *The complete list of stories and estimates. (Continued)*

Story	Estimate
A user can put books into a "wish list" that is visible to other site visitors.	2
A user, especially a Non-Sailing Gift Buyer, can search for a wish list based on its owner's name and state.	1
A user can check the status of her recent orders.	½
If an order hasn't shipped, a user can add or remove books, change the shipping method, the delivery address and the credit card.	1
A user can place an item from a wish list (even someone else's) into his or her shopping cart.	½
A repeat customer must be able to find one book and complete an order in less than 90 seconds.	0
A user can view a history of all of his past orders.	1
A user can easily re-purchase items when viewing past orders.	½
The site always tells a shopper what the last 3 (?) items she viewed are and provides links back to them. (This works even between sessions.)	1
A user can see what books we recommend on a variety of topics.	4
A user can choose to have items gift wrapped.	½
A user can choose to enclose a gift card and can write her own message for the card.	½
A Report Viewer can see reports of daily purchases broken down by book category, traffic, best- and worst-selling books and so on.	8
A user must be properly authenticated before viewing reports.	1
Orders made on the website have to end up in the same order database as telephone orders.	0
An administrator can add new books to the site.	1
An administrator can delete a book.	½
An administrator can edit the information about an existing book.	1
The system must support peak usage of up to 50 concurrent users.	0

Chapter 20

The Release Plan

The following steps are necessary in order to create the release plan:

1. Select an iteration length.

2. Estimate the velocity.

3. Prioritize the stories.

4. Allocate stories to the one or more iterations.

Because the new website features need to be available in four weeks, the team decides to use two-week iterations. This will give them the opportunity to run two iterations before the deadline. They'll prioritize the highest priority features into the first iteration to make sure those are completed. After the first iteration they will be able to assess their velocity and decide how much work they can bring into the second iteration.

Estimating Velocity

Maria and Rafe are will be the programmers on the project. Jay helped estimate but other commitments prevent him from helping develop the website. Since the project is unlike prior websites that the programmers have developed, they cannot estimate a velocity for the new project by basing it on the velocity of a prior project. So, they'll need to take an educated guess.

When they estimated the stories, Maria and Rafe loosely defined one story point as one ideal day of programming. They now decide that it will take them between two and three real days to do one ideal day worth of work. With two-week (ten-day) iterations and two programmers, there will be twenty programmer-days per iteration. Maria and Rafe estimate that they'll be able to complete between seven and ten story points during each iteration. Deciding to be conservative for the first iteration, they estimate velocity at eight.

Prioritizing the Stories

Lori the customer prioritizes the stories. The main factor in determining the priority of a story is the value it will deliver to the business. However, Lori also needs to consider the estimate for the story. Occasionally, highly desired stories become less desirable when their cost (the estimates) are considered.

To start prioritizing, Lori sorts the story cards into four piles based on their importance to the targeted go-live date in four weeks: Must Have, Should Have, Could Have, and Won't Have. Lori's Must-Have stories are shown in Table 20.1.

Table 20.1 *The Must-Have stories for the initial release in four weeks.*

Story	Estimate
A user can do a basic simple search that searches for a word or phrase in both the author and title fields.	1
A user can put books into a "shopping cart" and buy them when she is done shopping.	1
A user can remove books from her cart before completing an order.	½
To buy a book the user enters her billing address, the shipping address and credit card information.	2
A user can establish an account that remembers shipping and billing information.	2
Orders made on the website have to end up in the same order database as telephone orders.	0
An administrator can add new books to the site.	1
An administrator can delete a book.	½
An administrator can edit the information about an existing book.	1
The system must support peak usage of up to 50 concurrent users.	0

The sum of the estimates for Lori's must-have stories is nine. Since velocity is estimated at eight per iteration and there will be two iterations, this leaves room to dip into some of Lori's should-have stories. Lori pulls the stories shown in Table 20.2 from her pile of should-have stories. Between her must-have and should-have stories she's now identified 15½ points, which is close enough to the sixteen points the programmers think they can complete over two iterations.

Table 20.2 *The Should-Have stories Lori adds to the release plan.*

Story	Estimate
A user can search for books by entering values in any combination of author, title and ISBN.	1
A user can edit the credit card information stored in her account.	½
A user can edit the shipping and billing addresses stored in her account.	1
A user can see what books we recommend on a variety of topics.	4

The Finished Release Plan

The finished release plan is put together as shown in Table 20.3 and is communicated to the rest of the organization that way. Maria and Rafe will do their best to complete the work planned for the first iteration. If they do well, they'll work with Lori to move a new story or two up into the first iteration. If they get behind, they'll work with Lori to move a story or two from the first iteration to the second.

Table 20.3 *The finished release plan.*

Iteration 1	Iteration 2
A user can do a basic simple search that searches for a word or phrase in both the author and title fields.	An administrator can edit the information about an existing book.
A user can put books into a "shopping cart" and buy them when she is done shopping.	A user can search for books by entering values in any combination of author, title and ISBN.
A user can remove books from her cart before completing an order.	A user can edit the credit card information stored in her account.
To buy a book the user enters her billing address, the shipping address and credit card information.	A user can edit the shipping and billing addresses stored in her account.
Orders made on the website have to end up in the same order database as telephone orders.	A user can see what books we recommend on a variety of topics.

Table 20.3 *The finished release plan. (Continued)*

Iteration 1	Iteration 2
A user can establish an account that remembers shipping and billing information.	
An administrator can add new books to the site.	
An administrator can delete a book.	
The system must support peak usage of up to 50 concurrent users.	

Chapter 21

The Acceptance Tests

The acceptance tests for a story are used to determine whether the story is completed to the point where the customer can accept that part of the software as complete. This means that the customer is responsible for specifying the tests. Often, though, the customer will have some help from a tester who is assigned to the project. Since this project is small and without a dedicated tester, Lori enlists the help of Maria and Rafe. An additional benefit of this is that, beyond generating a list of acceptance tests, it leads to further conversations between Lori and the programmers.

The Search Tests

The search features that Lori prioritized into the first release are shown in Story Card 21.1 and Story Card 21.2. The tests for Story Card 21.1 are:

- Search for a word that is known to be part of a title but unlikely to be an author; for example, "navigation."

- Search for a word that is likely to be an author but unlikely to be a title; for example, "John."

- Search for a word that is unlikely to be in either; for example, "wookie."

A user can do a basic simple search that searches for a word or phrase in both the author and title fields.

◼ Story Card 21.1

The tests for Story Card 21.2 are:

- Use values for author and title that match at least one book.

- Use values for author and title that match no books.

- Try an ISBN search.

> A user can search for books by entering values in any combination of author, title and ISBN.

▩ Story Card 21.2

Shopping Cart Tests

Story Card 21.3 and Story Card 21.4 cover the use of the shopping cart.

> A user can put books into a "shopping cart" and buy them when she is done shopping.

▩ Story Card 21.3

> A user can remove books from her cart before completing an order.

▩ Story Card 21.4

Lori and the programmers talk about these stories and realize they have a few open questions: Can users put out-of-stock books into shopping carts? What about books that are not yet in print? Additionally, the team realizes that Story Card 21.4 covers changing the quantity of an item to 0, but there is no explicit story for increasing the quantity of an item. They could write this as a separate story but decide instead to rip up Story Card 21.4 and replaces it with Story Card 21.5.

An important result of this discussion is that the system has been simplified. By deciding they do not need a separate story deleting an item from a shopping

> A user can adjust the quantity of any item in her cart. Setting the quantity to 0 removes the item from the cart.

■ Story Card 21.5

cart the team has both improved the usabililty of the system and avoided potential future work.

The tests for Story Card 21.3 are:

- Put an out-of-stock book into the cart. Verify that the user is told that the book will be shipped when it becomes available.

- Put a book that hasn't been published yet into the cart. Verify that the user is told that the book will ship when available.

- Put a book that is in stock into the cart.

- Put a second copy of a book into the cart. Verify that the count goes up.

The tests for Story Card 21.5 are

- Change the quantity of a book from one to ten.

- Change the quantity from ten to one.

- Remove a book by changing the quantity to zero.

Buying Books

Story Card 21.6 covers the actual purchasing of books. In discussing this story, the programmers clarify a few aspects of it with Lori the customer. Lori wants users to be able to enter separate shipping and billing addresses or indicate that the addresses are the same. The site will accept only Visa and MasterCard.

> To buy a book the user enters her billing address, the shipping address and credit card information.

■ Story Card 21.6

The tests for Story Card 21.6 are:

- Enter a billing address and indicate that the shipping address is the same.

- Enter separate billing and shipping addresses.

- Test with a state and a postal code that is from another state and verify the inconsistency is caught.

- Verify that the address the books will ship to is the shipping address, not the billing address.

- Test with a valid Visa card.

- Test with a valid MasterCard.

- Test with a valid American Express card (fail).

- Test with an expired Visa.

- Test with a MasterCard that is over its credit limit.

- Test with a Visa that is missing digits.

- Test with a Visa with transposed digts.

- Test with a Visa with a completely invalid number.

User Accounts

Story Card 21.7 covers the creation of user accounts. Tests for this card are:

- Users can order without creating an account.

- Create an account then recall it and see if the information has been saved.

> A user can establish an account that remembers shipping and billing information.

■ Story Card 21.7

Story Card 21.8 and Story Card 21.9 allow users to modify the information stored in their accounts. Tests for Story Card 21.8 are:

- Edit the card number to make it an invalid number. Verify that the user is warned.

- Edit the expiration date to one in the past. Verify that the change isn't saved.

- Change the credit card number to a new valid number and make sure the change is saved.

- Change the expiration date to a date in the future and make sure the change is saved.

> A user can edit the credit card information stored in her account.

■ Story Card 21.8

Test for Story Card 21.9 are

- Change various parts of the shipping address and verify that the changes are saved.

- Change various parts of the billing address and verify that the changes are saved.

> A user can edit the shipping and billing addresses stored in her account.

■ Story Card 21.9

Administration

Story Card 21.10 allows an administrator to add new books to the site. Tests for this story are:

- Test that an administrator can add a book to the site.

- Test that a non-administrator cannot add a book.

- Test that a book can only be added if required data is present.

> An administrator can add new books to the site.

■ Story Card 21.10

Story Card 21.11 allows an administrator to delete a book. Tests for this story are:

- Verify that an administrator can delete a book.

- Verify that a non-administrator cannot delete a book.

- Delete a book and then verify that outstanding orders for the book will still ship.

> An administrator can delete a book.

■ Story Card 21.11

Story Card 21.12 allows an administrator to change information about a book. When the programmers and Lori discuss Story Card 21.12 they discuss how to handle unshipped orders that include a book for which the price changes. This becomes one of the tests for the story:

- Verify that items like name, author, number of pages, and so on,. can be changed.

- Verify that price can be changed but that price changes do not affect previously placed (but unbilled and unshipped orders).

> An administrator can edit the information about an existing book.

■ Story Card 21.12

Testing the Constraints

Among the stories Lori has prioritized into the release there are two constraints, which are shown as Story Card 21.13 and Story Card 21.14.

> Orders made on the website have to end up in the same order database as telephone orders.

■ Story Card 21.13

> The system must support peak usage of up to 50 concurrent users.

■ Story Card 21.14

The only test for Story Card 21.13 is to examine the database and verify that an order submitted from the website gets stored in the database:

- Place an order. Open up the telephone order entry database and verify that the order was stored in that database.

Lori takes Story Card 21.14, turns over the story card and writes:

- Test with fifty simulated users doing a variety of searches and placing orders. Ensure that no screen takes more than four seconds to display and that no orders are lost.

A Final Story

The only story left is shown on Story Card 21.15.

> A user can see what books we recommend on a variety of topics.

■ Story Card 21.15

Lori and the developers talk about Story Card 21.15 and decide it will be a simple static page that includes a list of recommendations for a variety of topics. They write these tests:

- Select a topic (for example, navigation or cruising) and view the recommendations for that topic. Make sure they make sense.

- Click on an item in the list to verify that the browser goes to a page of information on that book.

PART V

Appendices

You do not need to know much about Extreme Programming to read and benefit from this book. However, since user stories had their genesis in Extreme Programming, Appendix A provides a brief introduction to it. Appendix B contains answers to the questions that concluded most of the chapters.

Appendix A

An Overview of Extreme Programming

This appendix serves as a brief introduction to the main ideas of Extreme Programming (XP). If you are already familiar with XP you can safely skip this appendix. If not, please use this appendix as an introduction to XP and then proceed to one of the fine books that explain XP in detail.[1]

We'll look first at the people (or roles) involved in an XP project. Next we'll look at the twelve main practices of XP. We'll conclude by considering the values of an XP team.

Roles

The XP customer role is responsible for writing stories, prioritizing stories, and writing and executing tests that demonstrate that stories were developed as expected. The XP customer may be a user of the system being built but that is not necessary. If not a user, the XP customer is often a product manager, project manager or business analyst.

On some projects the customer role may actually be filled by a customer team, which would be composed of multiple highly interested individuals. The customer team will often include testers who assist with creating the acceptance tests. When a project has multiple customers, it is important that they speak with one voice. They can achieve this in many ways, but most commonly by designating one individual on the customer team as the first among equals.

---

1. In particular see *Extreme Programming Explained: Embrace change* (Beck 2000), *Extreme Programming Installed* (Jeffries, Anderson, and Hendrickson 2000), or *Extreme Programming Explored* (Wake 2002).

The XP programmer role encompasses a broad range of technical skills. XP projects tend not to draw distinctions between programmers, designers, database administrators, and so on. All programmers are expected to work as a team and to share many responsibilities that might otherwise be assigned to specific individuals on a non-XP project. Almost all processes expect programmers to unit test their code; XP takes this expectation seriously and programmers are expected to develop automated unit tests for everything they write.

Finally, many XP teams benefit from the use of an XP coach and possibly a project manager. The roles are sometimes combined within a single individual. The coach is responsible for monitoring the team's use of the XP practices and gently nudging them back on track when they stray. The project manager is more leader than manager and is responsible for sheltering the team from bureaucracy and removing as many obstacles as possible.

The Twelve Practices

Extreme Programming is characterized by the twelve practices described in Kent Beck's original "white book" (Beck 2000). If you choose to try XP on a project, you are highly encouraged to adopt all of the practices. XP's twelve practices are highly synergistic and interdependent. Practices support and enable each other. For example, the practice of refactoring is made easier by the practices of pair programming, simple design, collective ownership, continuous integration, and testing. The twelve practices are not a random collection of good ideas from which an XP team is allowed to pick their favorites. After becoming experienced with XP, you may choose to drop or alter a practice but you really should delay customizing XP until becoming experienced with standard XP.

In this appendix we will consider the following twelve XP practices:

- small releases
- the planning game
- refactoring
- testing
- pair programming
- sustainable pace
- team code ownership

- coding standard

- simple design

- metaphor

- continuous integration

- on-site customer

Small Releases

XP projects progress in a series of iterations, each of which is each typically one to three weeks long. Features, as described by user stories, are fully delivered within a single iteration. A team is not allowed to deliver half of a feature. Similarly, a team is not allowed to deliver the full feature but at half the quality. By the end of each iteration the team is responsible for delivering working, tested code that can immediately be put to use.

At the start of the project the team selects an iteration length that it will use for the duration of the project. The iteration length is typically one or two weeks and never longer than four. The team should select an iteration length that is as short as possible yet that will still deliver tangible value to the business. When undecided between two durations, choose the shorter one.

Iterations are firm timeboxes. A team cannot reach the planned last day of an iteration and and decide they need two more days. The iteration ends on the scheduled day. The amount of work the team does (but not the quality of that work) is adjusted to accommodate the iteration.

The Planning Game

The "Planning Game" is the XP name for release and iteration planning during which the developers and customer collaboratively make predictions about the future. Prior to initiating planning, the customer has written user stories on note cards and the developers have estimated the cost or magnitude of each story and have written the estimate on the story card.

To start planning, the developers estimate how much work they can complete in an iteration of the length selected for the project. The customer then looks over all of the story cards and selects her top priority stories for inclusion in the first iteration. She is allowed to select stories that sum to but do not exceed the amount of work the developers estimate they can do in the iteration. Once the first iteration is full of work, the customer moves onto selecting stories for the second and subsequent iterations.

After some number of iterations, the customer decides that enough stories have been placed into iterations that collectively they define a release. The release plan almost certainly does not accurately reflect what will be developed and in what order. The release plan is a hypothesis about how development may proceed but it will be updated at the start of each iteration as priorities change, as more becomes known about the rate of progress by the team, and as the developers learn more about the true expected costs of each story.

Prior to the start of each iteration, the team and customer plan the iteration. This involves selecting the highest priority stories that can be completed in the iteration and then identifying the specific tasks necessary to complete the story.

Refactoring

Refactoring (Fowler 1999; Wake 2003) refers to the restructuring or rewriting of code so as to improve the code without changing its external behavior. Over time code can get ugly. A method designed for one purpose is changed slightly to handle a special condition. Then, since it already handles that special condition, it's changed again to handle another special condition. And so on until the method becomes too fragile for further modification.

XP advocates constant attention to refactoring. Whenever a programmer makes a change to code that should be refactored, she is required to refactor it. She's not encouraged to refactor it; she's required to refactor it. In this way code avoids the slow, sometimes hard to detect decay that eventually results in obsolescence.

Refactoring is one of technique used by XP to replace upfront design. Rather than spending time upfront thinking through a system in advance of coding it, and therefore taking guesses at some aspects of its behavior, XP systems are refactored and kept in a state that perfectly meets known, implemented requirements.

Testing

An exciting practice of XP is its focus on testing. On an XP project the developers write automated unit tests and the customers write acceptance tests, which are often automated either by the customers themselves or with some help from the developers. Many XP developers have really found the benefits of early and frequent testing. Further, traditional resistance by developers to testing has gone down because XP unit tests are typically automated by writing test code that exercises the operational code—that is, even while testing they are programming.

In traditional development tests are written after the code (if they're written at all). This becomes a problem because once code is written and appears to work, it can be human nature not to push too hard on the code. So, many developers push gently on their code and call it tested. (I know this: I used to be one of them.) XP changes this and puts the tests right up front in a practice called *test-driven development* (Beck 2003; Astels 2003).

In test-driven development, tests are written before the code. Developers follow a short (minutes, not hours) cycle of test–code–test–code and so on. They follow a rule that no operational code may be written except in response to a failing test. So, they write a test that fails. The program is run to verify that the test fails. Only then does a programmer write the code that makes the program pass the test.

Test-driven development guarantees that code will remain well factored and testable. It also leads to more maintainable code since code is effectively in a maintenance mode right from the start.

In addition to programmer unit testing, customer tests are an important part of XP. For each story, the customer is responsible for defining a series of tests that are used to determine if the story was developed in accordance with the customer's expectations and assumptions. In many ways, these customer-written acceptance tests replace the requirements documents of a waterfall process.

Pair Programming

One of XP's more controversial practices is pair programming. Pair programming refers to two programmers sharing one keyboard and one monitor but using their two brains to write code. While one programmer is typing at the keyboard (and mentally thinking a few lines ahead in his code), the second programmer is watching the code develop and thinking more broadly about where the code may lead and what problems it may encounter. Pairs switch roles and partners often.

While pair programming may sound tremendously inefficient, Alistair Cockburn and Laurie Williams (2001) have studied it and found that not to be the case. They found that for a 15% increase in total programming time, pair programming leads to:

- lower defect counts

- less code is written to solve the same problem

- problems being solved more quickly

- more people understand each piece of code

- an increase in developer job satisfaction

Pair programming is important to XP because so many of the other XP practices require discipline. It requires a tremendous amount of discipline to refactor every time you notice poorly structured code or to always write tests before writing operational code. Without a pair it can be far too tempting to skip a refactoring or a test with the thought of "Just this once…"

Sustainable Pace

XP teams are encouraged to work at a sustainable pace. The belief is that an XP team moving at a consistent but brisk pace will achieve more over a period of time than will a team working at a pace they cannot sustain over a long period. This does not mean that an XP team works exactly forty hours each week and then heads for home. It is up to the team to determine their sustained pace, and it is likely to be different for different members of the team.

Pair programming and test-driven development are effective because they focus the minds of the pair very intensely on the code they are creating. Few people are capable of maintaining this level of intensity for extended periods. A team will typically devote around six hours per day to pairing and spend the remainder of the day in other activities.

An XP coach is responsible for monitoring the team for burnout. If the coach senses a team is burning out she will help the team shift back to working at a sustainable pace.

Team Code Ownership

It has been common among non-XP teams for individual developers to "own" or assume full responsiblity for portions of a system's code. In this way each portion of a system would be owned by one developer—at least until a developer moves onto another project and her code is left without an owner. This view toward code ownership also leads teams to make comments such as "We can't change the billing source code until Eli gets back from vacation." Further, if a developer is talked into changing the code while Eli is on vacation, Eli will probably be angry about changes made to "his code" when he returns.

XP teams take a completely different approach to code ownership: All code is owned by everyone. Under this model of team ownership, any pair of developers can change any code. In fact, because of the refactoring practice, pairs are expected to change code they didn't write.

Individual ownership is practiced to ensure coherent design and to keep all responsibilities of a module balanced. In XP, this burden is borne by test-driven development. A strong suite of unit tests ensures that changes do not introduce unanticipated side effects.

Coding Standards

Because XP teams collectively own their source code, it is important that they follow a coding standard. The coding standard lays out the main rules and conventions team members will follow when writing code: how will variables and methods be named? how will lines be formatted? and so on.

A small, close-knit team may be able to get by without a written, formalized coding standard. They can build and share standards through team folklore. Beyond a handful of developers, most teams will benefit from writing down their coding standards but still keeping them as brief and essential as possible.

Simple Design

XP teams pursue a goal of having the simplest possible design that delivers the features a customer needs. Kent Beck (2000) defines four constraints that indicate when a design is the simplest it can be:

1. The operational code and the test code fully convey the programmer's intent for the behavior of that code.

2. There is no duplicated code.

3. The system uses the least number of classes.

4. The system uses the least number of methods.

Metaphor

XP teams support the quest for simple design by finding a metaphor that can be used for the whole system. The metaphor provides a frame of reference for how they think about the system. For example, on one project our metaphor was that the system was like a chalkboard and that various parts of the system could write on the chalkboard. When the user was done with the system she would either save the contents of the chalkboard or erase them. This greatly simplified way of thinking about the system helped us by giving us a convenient, simple way of thinking about the behavior of the system.

Continuous Integration

I got involved in a discussion recently with an executive at one of the largest eCommerce companies. He told that me that integrating the work of multiple developers was the largest problem for most software development teams. He liked to have his teams integrate their software once a month so they could avoid the bigger problems of integrating less frequently. I asked him what would happen if his teams instead integrated on a daily basis.

XP teams know the answer and they integrate at least daily. We learned long ago about the benefits of a daily build and smoke test (Cusumano and Selby 1995). XP teams have taken this to the point where code is integrated more or less continuously. For example, a developer completes a small change, she checks the change into the source code repository where a process notices the change and initiates a full build. When the build is complete a suite of automated tests is run. If any of the tests fail, the developer is emailed and told about the failure. Integration problems are fixed one at a time in extremely small batches as soon as they occur.

On-Site Customer

It used to be common for a customer to write a requirements document, throw it over a wall to the programmers who would write the code and then throw the system over another wall to some testers. With XP the walls are gone and the customer is expected to sit with and be part of the development team. The customer writes the stories and the acceptance tests and also is on hand to answer questions as soon as they arise.

The on-site customer is essential to successful use of the user story approach because of the many conversations that must occur between the customer and the developers. If the customer is not on site, delays will disrupt the predictable progress of the XP team.

XP's Values

In addition to its practices, XP advocates four values: communication, simplicity, feedback and courage. XP values communication but not all modes of communication are equal. Most desirable is face–to–face communication where we can talk, respond, gesture and draw on a whiteboard. Less desirable are written documents. XP stresses communication through practices such as pair programming.

Simplicity is a value of XP teams because it keeps their focus on creating a solution to the problem faced today, not the problem anticipated tomorrow. XP teams do not architect a system with support for features beyond those that are necessary for developing the features of the current iteration. They remain constantly focused on doing the simplest thing that could possibly work.

XP teams value feedback, and the more immediate the feedback the better. XP developers give and get feedback during pair programming when one developer points out a potential problem to her pair. They get feedback from the automated tests they run so often. They get feedback from their continuous (or at least daily) integration process. Customers are part of the team, even sitting in the same space with the developers, and provide feedback through constant interaction with the team and through the acceptance tests they write.

Finally, XP teams value courage. For example, they have courage to refactor their code (because they have automated tests to back up that courage). They have courage to proceed without an overall master architecture because they will use a metaphor and maintain a simple design through refactoring and test-driven development.

The Principles of XP

In addition to its values and practices, XP can be characterized by its five basic principles: rapid feedback, assuming simplicity, incremental change, embracing change, and doing quality work (Beck 2000). Since the introduction of XP, a debate has raged over whether a team can be doing XP if they doing only eleven of the original twelve practices. Is a team that doesn't pair program doing XP? Is a team that pursues a simple design but starts with a few weeks of modeling doing XP?

I think the answer is yes. These teams are doing XP if they are living by the principles of XP. A team that:

- provides rapid feedback to its customers and learns from that feedback

- favors simplicity and always attempts a simple solution before moving to a more complex one

- improves the software through small, incremental changes

- embraces change because they know they are truly adept at accommodating and adapting

- and, insists that the software consistently exhibits the highest level of quality workmanship

must certainly be doing XP, even if they missing a practice or two.

Summary

- The XP customer role is responsible for writing stories and acceptance tests for each story, and sits with the development team.

- On an XP project the distinction between programmer and tester is blurred. Programmers write unit tests of their own code; testers program automated acceptance tests.

- XP projects include a coach and possibly a separate project manager who are responsible for guiding the team and removing obstacles from its way.

Extreme Programming involves the following practices:

- small releases
- the planning game
- refactoring
- testing
- pair programming
- sustainable pace
- collective code ownership
- coding standard
- simple design
- metaphor
- continuous integration
- on-site customer

And has these values:

- communication
- simplicity

- feedback

- courage

And has these key principles:

- rapid feedback

- assume simplicity

- incremental change

- embrace change

- quality work

Appendix B

Answers to Questions

Chapter 1, An Overview

1.1. What are the three parts of a user story?
Answer: Card, Conversation, and Confirmation.

1.2. Who is on the customer team?
Answer: The customer team includes those who ensure that the software will meet the needs of its intended users. This may include testers, a product manager, real users, and interaction designers.

1.3. Which of the following are not good stories? Why?
Answer: See Table B.1.

Table B.1 *Answer to Question 1.3.*

Story	Answer
a. The user can run the system on Windows XP and Linux.	This is a good story.
b. All graphing and charting will be done using a third-party library.	This is not a good story. Users will not care how the graphing and charting are done.
c. The user can undo up to fifty commands.	This is a good story.
d. The software will be released by June 30.	This is not a good story. It is a constraint that will need to be considered during release planning.
e. The software will be written in Java.	This is probably not a good story but it depends on the product. If the product is a class library being marketed to Java programmers, those users will care about the language.

Table B.1 *Answer to Question 1.3. (Continued)*

Story	Answer
f. The user can select her country from a drop-down list.	This is a good story but it may be a little small.
g. The system will use Log4J to log all error messages to a file.	This is not a good story as written. It should not specify that Log4J be used as the logging mechanism.
h. The user will be prompted to save her work if she hasn't saved it for 15 minutes.	This is a good story.
i. The user can select an "Export to XML" feature.	This is a good story.
j. The user can export data to XML.	This is a good story.

1.4. What advantages do requirements conversations have over requirements documents?

> *Answer:* Written documents imply a precision that they can't back. User stories, with cards as reminders to hold conversations, avoid the false appearance of being highly precise. Writing things down is no guarantee that customers will get what they want; at best customers will get what was written down. Frequent conversations, especially ones close to and during development of the feature being discussed, lead to greater and shared understanding between the developers and customers.

1.5. Why would you want to write tests on the back of a story card?

> *Answer:* Writing tests on the back of a card is a great way for the customer to communicate her expectations and assumptions about a story.

Chapter 2, Writing Stories

2.1. For the following stories, indicate if it is a good story or not. If not, why?
> *Answer:* See Table B.2.

2.2. Break this epic up into appropriately sized component stories: "A user can make and change automated job search agents."
> *Answer:* Minimally this epic should be split into two stories, one to make and one to change agents. However, it could be split many different ways, depending on how long the stories are likely to take to implement. One possible disaggregation is:
> - A user can make an automated job search agent.

- A user can edit the search parameters of an automated job search agent.

- A user can change the times when an automated job search agent will run.

- A user can change how the results of an automated job search agent will be reported.

Table B.2 *Answer to Question 2.1.*

Story	Answer
a. A user can quickly master the system.	This story should be changed. Neither "quickly" nor "master" is defined.
b. A user can edit the address on a resume.	This story is probably too small, but it could be OK depending on how long it would likely take the developers to implement.
c. A user can add, edit and delete multiple resumes.	This is a compound story and should be split into multiple stories.
d. The system can calculate saddlepoint approximations for distributions of quadratic forms in normal variables.	If the customer wrote this story then she probably knows what it means. However, if the developers don't understand this story then the customer should consider rewriting it (or at least having a good conversation about it) so that the developers can estimate it.
e. All runtime errors are logged in a consistent manner.	This story is fine as is.

Chapter 3, User Role Modeling

3.1. Take a look at the eBay website. What user roles can you identify?

   Answer: Your list should include some roles similar to these: One-time Seller, Small Seller, Frequent Seller, Infrequent Buyer, Frequent Buyer, Corporate Seller, Manufacturer, Payment Processor, Collector, Club Member, Software Developer, Affiliate, Wireless Seller, Wireless Buyer

3.2. Consolidate the roles you came up with in the previous question and show how you would lay out the role cards. Explain your answer.

   Answer: From my list, I consolidated sellers into a generic Seller role and three more specialized sellers: Small Seller, Frequent Seller and

Corporate Seller. Similarly, I had a generic Buyer role specialized into Infrequent Buyer, Frequent Buyer and Collector. I also kept Payment Processor, Affiliate and a generic Wireless User.

3.3. Write persona descriptions for the one most important user role.

    Answer: Brenda is a Frequent Buyer. During a typical week she visits the site at least once a day, and makes an average of one or two purchases per week. She typically buys movies and books but she has also purchased gardening and kitchen items. She is a realtor and is very comfortable on our site but is a little uncomfortable learning most new software. She usually accesses the site from her dial-up connection at home but occasionally accesses it from her faster office connection.

Chapter 4, Gathering Stories

4.1. What problems would you expect if a team only gathered requirements through the use of questionnaires?

    Answer: Questionnaires can take a long time to turn around so the project will take longer to complete. Someone will need to aggregate and interpret the results, which means there will be some degree of misinterpretation. Because questionnaires do not provide for true two-way communication, it will be extremely hard for a team to get feedback as to whether it's on the right track.

4.2. Rephrase the following questions to be context free and open-ended. Do you think the user should have to enter a password? Should the system automatically save the user's work every 15 minutes? Can one user see database entries saved by another user?

    Answer: There are many ways to reword these. Here are some examples:

- Describe how the system should safeguard sensitive data.

- What would a user do if the system crashed while she was using it?

- Tell me about the accessibility of data saved by a user.

4.3. Why is it best to ask open-ended, context-free questions?

    Answer: Context-free questions do not imply an answer ("When did you stop beating your wife?") so the respondent does not feel a need to give the "right" answer. Open-ended questions allow detailed responses that go beyond a simple yes or no. Open-ended, context-free questions are best because they do not influence the response and they allow a broader range of responses than yes or no.

Chapter 5, Working with User Proxies

5.1. What problems can result from using the users' manager as a proxy for the users?

Answer: Even if the users' manager is a current user of the software, her needs almost certainly differ from the needs of the users. Worse, if she is a former user, her knowledge of the system is outdated.

5.2. What problems can result from using a domain expert as a proxy for users?

Answer: One problem is that the domain expert may not be a user of the system. If she is, her use of the system may differ from less expert users. A second problem is that you may end up with a system that is perfect for experts, but that is not usable by those with less than expert level domain knowledge.

Chapter 6, Acceptance Testing User Stories

6.1. Who specifies the tests? Who helps?

Answer: The customer specifies the tests. The customer will usually work with a programmer or tester to actually create the tests, but minimally the customer needs to specify the tests that will be used to know when a story has been correctly developed.

6.2. Why specify tests before the stories are coded?

Answer: Tests are specified before coding begins because they are a useful and effective method for communicating the customer's assumptions about the new functionality.

Chapter 7, Guidelines for Good Stories

7.1. Assume the story "A Job Seeker can search for open jobs" is too large to fit into one iteration. How would you split it?

Answer: This story can probably be split based on the search parameters supported such as location, key words, job title, salary, and so on. Additionally, there may be different ways to present the results.

An initial story might cover a very simple list of each matched job. That story could be augmented by a story to enhance the display of the results, perhaps with more details about each job, allowing the user to select a sort order or what fields are displayed, or providing a link to more details about the job.

7.2. Which of these stories is appropriately sized and can be considered a closed story?
    Answer: See Table B.3.

Table B.3 *Answer to question 7.2.*

Story	Answer
a. A user can save her preferences.	This story may or may not be closed, depending on the system. If saving preferences is something a user may want to do, it can probably be considered closed. It might be on the small side but is probably OK, again depending on the system and the team building it.
b. A user can change the default credit card used for purchases.	This is a closed and appropriately sized story.
c. A user can log on to the system.	This story is not closed and is probably too small.

7.3. What simple changes could improve the story "Users can post their resumes"?
    Answer: As written, it is not clear if a user can post multiple resumes. This undoubtedly will come out during conversations about the story, but it is better to write the story more clearly as "A Job Seeker can post one or more resumes."

7.4. How would you test the constraint "The software will be easy to use"?
    Answer: In order to test this, you must first define what "easy to use" means. Does it mean that a skilled user can complete common tasks with a minimum number of keystrokes? Or does it mean that a new user can quickly achieve a given level of proficiency with the software? Most commonly it will mean the latter. If so, define one or more tests such as:

- A new user can search for a job, register on the system, and post her resume within 30 minutes of first seeing the system.

Tests like these can't be performed as part of a project's nightly builds, but they can be verified by occasioanal usability testing during which new users are shown the software and observed.

Chapter 8, Estimating User Stories

8.1. During an estimating meeting three programmers are estimating a story.
Individually they estimate the story at two, four and five story points.
Which estimate should they use?

   Answer: They should continue discussing the story until their estimates get
   closer.

8.2. What is the purpose of triangulating estimates?

   Answer: Triangulation improves estimates by making sure that each estimate makes sense in relation to multiple other estimates. If a two-
   point story seems to be twice a one-point story, it should also
   seem to be one-half of a four-point story.

8.3. Define velocity.

   Answer: Velocity is the number of story points completed by a team in an
   iteration.

8.4. Team A finished 43 story points in their last two-week iteration. Team B is
working on a separate project and has twice as many developers. They
also completed 43 story points in their last two-week iteration. How can
that be?

   Answer: The story points of one team are not comparable to the story
   points of any other team. From the information in this question,
   we cannot infer that Team A is twice as productive as Team B.

Chapter 9, Planning a Release

9.1. What are three ways of estimating a team's initial velocity?

   Answer: You can use historical values, take a guess, or run an initial iteration and use the velocity of that iteration.

9.2. Assuming one-week iterations and a team of four developers, how many
iterations will it take the team to complete a project with 27 story points
if they have a velocity of 4?

   Answer: With a velocity of 4 and 27 story points in the project, it will take
   the team 7 iterations to finish.

Chapter 10, Planning an Iteration

10.1. Disaggregate this story into its constituent tasks: A user can view detailed information about a hotel.

Answer: There are, of course, many ways to do this, but here's one:

- Design the look of these web pages.
- Code the HTML to display hotel and room photos.
- Code the HTML to display a map showing where the hotel is.
- Code the HTML to display a list of hotel amenities and services.
- Figure out how we're generating maps.
- Write SQL to retrieve information from the database.
- And so on.

Chapter 11, Measuring and Monitoring Velocity

11.1. A story estimated at one story point actually took two days to complete. How much does it contribute to velocity when calculated at the end of the iteration?

Answer: It contributes one point.

11.2. What can you learn from a daily burndown chart that you can't see on an iteration burndown chart?

Answer: Daily burndown charts show the progress of the team during the iteration. You can use this information to gauge whether all planned work will be completed by the end of the iteration. If it becomes apparent that not all work can be completed, the team and customer can talk during the iteration about which work should be deferred.

11.3. What conclusions should you draw from Figure 11.7? Does the project look like it will finish ahead, behind or on schedule?

Answer: This team started out a little better than anticipated in the first iteration. They expected velocity to improve in the second and third iterations and then stabilize. After two iterations they have already achieved the velocity they expected after three iterations. At this point they are ahead of schedule but you should be reluctant to draw too many firm conclusions after only two iterations.

11.4. What is the velocity of the team that finished the iteration shown in Table 11.3?

Answer: Sixteen. Partially completed stories do not contribute to velocity.

11.5. What circumstances would cause an iteration burndown chart to reflect an upward trend?

Answer: An iteration burndown chart will trend upwards if new work is being added faster than known work is being completed, or if the team decides that a significant amount of future work has been underestimated.

11.6. Complete Table 11.4 by writing the missing values into the table.

Answer: The completed table appears as Table B.4.

Table B.4 *Answer to question 11.6.*

	Iteration 1	Iteration 2	Iteration 3
Story points at start of iteration	100	76	34
Completed during iteration	35	40	36
Changed estimates	5	−5	0
Story points from new stories	6	3	2
Story points at end of iteration	76	34	0

Chapter 12, What Stories Are Not

12.1. What are the key differences between user stories and use cases?

Answer: A user story usually encompasses a smaller scope than a use case. User stories do not include as much detail as use cases. User stories are not intended to be useful after the iteration in which they are developed; use cases are often intended as permanent artifacts of a project.

12.2. What are the key differences between user stories and IEEE 830 requirements statements?

Answer: IEEE 830-style requirements statements focus on the attributes of the solution, while user stories focus on the user's goals. IEEE 830 requirements specifications encourage teams to write all of the requirements statements up front rather than in an iterative manner, as with user stories. Great care is taken in writing requirements statements to make sure the words convey the proper meaning; user stories acknowledge the superiority of conversations for clarifying details.

12.3. What are the key differences between user stories and interaction design scenarios?

    Answer: Interaction design scenarios are much more detailed than user stories, often describing the persona and the context of the system use in great detail. Also, a scenario often describes a broader scope than does a user story.

12.4. For a non-trivial project, why is it impossible to write all the requirements at the start of the project?

    Answer: Attempting to write all requirements at the start of a project ignores an important feedback loop. When a system's intended users begin to see and interact with the system, new requirements come to mind.

12.5. What is the advantage to thinking about users' goals rather than on listing the attributes of the software to be built?

    Answer: A list of attributes does not give the reader the same overall understanding of a product that stories and conversations do. Also, if our work is driven by a list of product attributes, when we are done the best we can say is that the delivered product possesses the attributes on the list. This is not the same as saying the delivered product meets all of a user's goals.

Chapter 13, Why User Stories?

13.1. What are four good reasons for using user stories to express requirements?

    Answer: User stories emphasize verbal communication, are comprehensible by everyone, are the right size for planning, support iterative development, encourage deferring detail, support opportunistic design, encourage participatory design and build up tacit knowledge.

13.2. What can be two drawbacks to using user stories?

    Answer: On large projects it can be difficult to keep hundreds or thousands of stories organized; stories may need to be augmented with additional documents for traceability; and, while great at improving tacit knowledge through face-to-face communication, conversations do not scale adequately to entirely replace written documents on large projects.

13.3. What is the key difference between participatory and empirical design?

    Answer: In participatory design, the intended users of a system become a part of the team designing the behavior of that system. In empirical design, the intended users are instead studied or observed by the designers of the software, who then make all of the design decisions.

13.4. What is wrong with the requirements statement, "All multipage reports should be numbered"?

Answer: It is unclear what "should be numbered" means. Does this mean that the programmers should code this functionality but don't have to? Does it mean pages should be numbered if there's room on the page?

Chapter 14, A Catalog of Story Smells

14.1. What should you do if the team is consistently finding it difficult to plan the next iteration?

Answer: There could be other reasons but you should consider whether too many stories are interdependent, or are too small or too large.

14.2. What should the team do if they are consistently running out of room to write on the story cards?

Answer: They should use smaller cards to enforce the discipline of keeping details out of the story descriptions.

14.3. What could cause the customer to have a difficult time prioritizing stories?

Answer: The stories may be the wrong size (either too large or too small) or the stories may not clearly express value to users or customers.

14.4. How do you know if you are splitting too many stories?

Answer: You have to rely on your gut feel. Stories are often and legitimately split because they were intentionally written as epics to start with, or because they are too big to fit into an iteration. If you find yourself frequently splitting stories for other reasons, you may be doing it too often.

Chapter 15, Using Stories with Scrum

15.1. Describe the differences between an incremental and an iterative process.

Answer: An iterative process is one that makes progress through successive refinement. An incremental process is one in which software is built and delivered in pieces.

15.2. What is the relationship between the product backlog and the sprint backlog?

Answer: Items are moved from the product backlog to the sprint backlog at the start of a sprint.

15.3. What is meant by a potentially shippable product increment?

Answer: By the end of each sprint a Scrum team is responsible for creating a potentially shippable product increment. This means the software is coded, tested and could be given to users.

15.4. Who is responsible for prioritizing work and for selecting the work the team will perform during a sprint?

Answer: The Product Owner prioritizes the work but the team selects the work they will perform during a sprint. Naturally they are expected to select from among the top priority items.

15.5. What questions are answered by each team member at the daily scrum?

Answer: What did you do yesterday? What will you do today? What is in your way?

Chapter 16, Additional Topics

16.1. How should you handle a requirement for a system to scale up to use by 1,000 concurrent users?

Answer: You should write this as a constraint and then supplement it with appropriate tests. Depending on the system, you may want to start with a test for 100 concurrent users in one iteration and progressively increase that to 1,000 users over a number of iterations.

16.2. Do you prefer to write stories on note cards or in a software system? Defend your answer.

Answer: The low-tech simplicity of note cards make them ideal for many projects. Cards also offer a limited amount of space, which helps keep stories brief. Because they can be easily shuffled about on a table or wall they are ideal for planning. However, a team that is not collocated or has stringent traceability requirements might prefer to work with software.

16.3. What impact does an iterative process have on the user interface of an application?

Answer: Iterative refinement of the system can make it harder for users to learn the system. When menu systems change or features appear in different places, users must relearn they system.

16.4. Give some examples of systems that could benefit from more upfront consideration of the user interface than is typically given on an agile project.

   Answer: There can be many examples but here are a few:

   - a commercial product that competes in a mature industry primarily through ease of use

   - software aimed at novice users

   - software that will be used rarely but for intense periods (such as for income tax preparation)

   - software for low vision users or users with a movement disorder

References

Books and Articles

Adolph, Steve, Paul Bramble, et al. *Patterns for Effective Use Cases.* Reading, Mass.: Addison-Wesley, 2002.

Antón, Annie I., and Colin Potts. "The Use of Goals to Surface Requirements for Evolving Systems," in Proceedings of the 20th International Conference on Software Engineering (ICSE 98), April 1998: 157–166.

Astels, Dave. *Test Driven Development: A practical guide.* Upper Saddle River, N.J.: Prentice Hall, 2003.

Beck, Kent. *Extreme Programming Explained: Embrace change.* Boston: Addison-Wesley, 2000.

———. *Test Driven Development.* Reading, Mass.: Addison-Wesley, 2003.

Beck, Kent, and Martin Fowler. *Planning Extreme Programming.* Reading, Mass.: Addison-Wesley, 2000.

Beedle, Mike, et al. "SCRUM: A Pattern Language for Hyperproductive Software Development." In Neil Harrison et al. (Eds.), *Pattern Languages of Program Design 4.* Addison-Wesley: 1999, pp. 637–651.

Boehm, Barry. "A Spiral Model of Development and Enhancement." *IEEE Computer 28,* no. 5 (May 1988): 61–72.

———. *Software Engineering Economics.* Englewood Cliffs, N.J.: Prentice-Hall, 1981.

Bower, G. H., J. B. Black, and T. J. Turner. "Scripts in Memory for Text." *Cognitive Psychology 11* (1979): 177–220.

Carroll, John M. "Making Use a Design Representation." *Communications of the ACM 37,* no. 12 (December 1994): 29–35.

———. *Making Use: Scenario-based design in human-computer interaction.* Cambridge, Mass.: The MIT Press, 2000.

———. "Making use is more than a matter of task analysis." *Interacting with Computers 14,* no. 5 (2002): 619–627.

259

Carroll, John M., Mary Beth Rosson, George Chin Jr., and Jürgen Koenemann. "Requirements Development in Scenario-Based Design." *IEEE Transactions on Software Engineering 24*, no. 12 (December 1998): 1156–1170.

Cirillo, Francesco. "XP: Delivering the Competitive Edge in the Post-Internet Era." At www.communications.xplabs.com/paper2001-3.html. XP Labs, 2001.

Cockburn, Alistair. *Writing Effective Use Cases.* Upper Saddle River, N.J.: Addison-Wesley, 2001.

Cockburn, Alistair, and Laurie L. Williams. "The Costs and Benefits of Pair Programming." In Giancarlo Succi and Michele Marchesi (Eds.), *Extreme Programming Examined.* Upper Saddle River, N.J.: Addison-Wesley, 2001.

Cohn, Mike. "The Upside of Downsizing." *Software Test and Quality Engineering 5*, no. 1 (January 2003): 18–21.

Constantine, Larry. "Cutting Corners." Software Development (February 2000).

———. "Process Agility and Software Usability: Toward lightweight and usage-centered design." *Information Age* (August-September 2002).

Constantine, Larry L., and Lucy A. D. Lockwood. *Software for Use: A practical guide to the models and methods of usage-centered design.* Reading, Mass.: Addison-Wesley, 1999.

———. "Usage-Centered Engineering for Web Applications." *IEEE Software 19*, no. 2 (March/April 2002): 42–50.

Cooper, Alan. *The Inmates Are Running the Asylum.* Indianapolis: SAMS, 1999.

Cusumano, Michael A., and Richard W. Selby. *Microsoft Secrets: How the world's most powerful software company creates technology, shapes markets, and manages people.* New York: The Free Press, 1995.

Davies, Rachel. "The Power of Stories." XP 2001. Sardinia, 2001.

Djajadiningrat, J.P., W. W. Gaver and J. W. Frens. "Interaction Relabelling and Extreme Characters: Methods for exploring aesthetic interactions." *Symposium on Designing Interactive Systems 2000,* 2000: 66–71.

Fowler, Martin. "The Almighty Thud." *Distributed Computing* (November 1997).

Fowler, Martin, et al. *Refactoring: Improving the design of existing code*, Reading, Mass.: Addison-Wesley, 1999.

Gilb, Tom. *Principles of Software Engineering Management.* Reading, Mass.: Addison-Wesley, 1988.

Guindon, Raymonde. "Designing the Design Process: Exploiting opportunistic thoughts." *Human-Computer Interaction 5*, 1990.

Grudin, Jonathan, and John Pruitt. "Personas, Participatory Design and Product Development: An Infrastructure for Engagement." In Thomas Binder, Judith Gregory, and Ina Wagner (Eds.), *Participation and Design: Inquiring into the politics, contexts and practices of collaborative design work, Proceedings of the Participatory Design Conference 2002*: 2002: 144–161.

IEEE Computer Society. *IEEE Recommended Practice for Software Requirements Specifications*. New York, 1998.

Jacobson, Ivar. *Object-Oriented Software Engineering*. Upper Saddle River, N.J.: Addison-Wesley, 1992.

Jacobson, Ivar, Grady Booch, and James Rumbaugh. *The Unified Software Development Process*. Reading, Mass: Addison-Wesley, 1999.

Jeffries, Ron. "Essential XP: Card, Conversation, and Confirmation." *XP Magazine* (August 30, 2001).

Jeffries, Ron, Ann Anderson, and Chet Hendrickson. *Extreme Programming Installed*. Boston: Addison-Wesley, 2000.

Kensing, Finn, and Andreas Munk-Madsen. "PD: Structure in the Toolbox." *Communications of the ACM 36*, no. 6 (June 1993): 78–85.

Kovitz, Ben L. *Practical Software Requirements: A manual of content and style*. Greenwich, Conn.: Manning, 1999.

Kuhn, Sarah, and Michael J. Muller. "Introduction to the Special Section on Participatory Design." *Communications of the ACM 36*, no. 6 (June 1993): 24–28.

Lauesen, Soren. *Software Requirements: Styles and techniques*. London: Addison-Wesley, 2002.

Lundh, Erik, and Martin Sandberg. "Time Constrained Requirements Engineering with Extreme Programming: An experience report." In Armin Eberlein and Julio Cesar Sampaio do Prado Leite (Eds.), *Proceedings of the International Workshop on Time Constrained Requirements Engineering*, 2002.

Newkirk, James, and Robert C. Martin. *Extreme Programming in Practice*. Upper Saddle River, N.J.: Addison-Wesley, 2001.

Parnas, David L., and Paul C. Clements. "A Rational Design Process: How and why to fake it." *IEEE Transactions on Software Engineering 12*, no. 2 (February 1986): 251–7.

Patton, Jeff. "Hitting the Target: Adding interaction design to agile software development." Conference on Object Oriented Programming Systems Languages and Applications (OOPSLA 2002). New York: ACM Press, 2002.

Poppendieck, Tom. *The Agile Customer's Toolkit*. In Larry L. Constantine (Ed.), *Proceedings of forUSE 2003*. Rowley, Mass.: Ampersand Press: 2003.

Potts, Colin, Kenji Takahashi, and Annie I. Antón. "Inquiry-Based Requirements Analysis." *IEEE Software 11*, no. 2 (March/April 1994): 21–32.

Robertson, Suzanne and James Robertson. *Mastering the Requirements Process*. Reading, Mass.: Addison-Wesley, 1999.

Schuler, Douglas, and Aki Namioka (Eds.). *Participatory Design: Principles and practices*. Hillsdale, N.J.: Erlbaum, 1993.

Schwaber, Ken, and Mike Beedle. *Agile Software Development with Scrum*. Upper Saddle River, N.J.: Prentice Hall, 2002.

Stapleton, Jennifer. *DSDM: Business Focused Development*. Reading, Mass.: Addison-Wesley, 2003.

Swartout, William, and Robert Balzer. "On the Inevitable Intertwining of Specification and Implementation." *Communications of the ACM 25*, no. 7 (July 1982): 438–440.

Wagner, Larry. "Extreme Requirements Engineering." *Cutter IT Journal 14*, no. 12 (December 2001).

Wake, William C. *Extreme Programming Explored*. Reading, Mass: Addison-Wesley, 2002.

———. "INVEST in Good Stories, and SMART Tasks." At www.xp123.com, 2003a.

———. *Refactoring Workbook*. Reading, Mass.: Addison-Wesley, 2003b.

Weidenhaupt, Klaus, Klaus Pohl, Matthias Jarke, and Peter Haumer. "Scenarios in System Development: Current practice." *IEEE Software 15*, no. 2 (March/April 1998): 34–45.

Wiegers, Karl E. *Software Requirements*. Redmond, Wash.: Microsoft Press, 1999.

Williams, Marian G., and Vivienne Begg. "Translation between software designers and users." *Communications of the ACM 36*, no. 6 (June 1993): 102–3.

Websites

www.agilealliance.com
www.controlchaos.com
www.foruse.com
www.mountaingoatsoftware.com
www.userstories.com
www.xprogramming.com
www.xp123.com

Index

Printed in Great Britain
by Amazon